Great Meals in Minutes was created by Rebus, Inc.
and published by Time-Life Books.

Rebus, Inc.

Publisher: Rodney Friedman
Editor: Shirley Tomkievicz
Executive Editor: Elizabeth P. Rice
Art Director: Ronald Gross
Senior Editors: Brenda Goldberg,
Ruth A. Peltason
Food Editor and Food Stylist: Grace Young
Photographer: Steven Mays
Prop Stylist: Zazel Wilde Lovén
Staff Writer: Alexandra Greeley
Editorial Assistants: Donna Kalvarsky,
Michael Flint
Photography, Styling Assistant: Cathryn
Schwing
Editorial Board: Angelica Cannon, Sally
Dorst, Lilyan Glusker, Kim MacArthur,
Valerie Marchant, Joan Whitman

For information about any Time-Life book,
please write:
Reader Information
Time-Life Books
541 North Fairbanks Court
Chicago, Illinois 60611

Library of Congress Cataloging in Publication Data
Vegetable menus.
    (Great meals in minutes)
    Includes index.
    1. Cookery (Vegetables) 2. Cooks—United States—
      Biography.
I. Time-Life Books. II. Title. III. Series.
TX801.V4175 1984   642   83-9322
ISBN 0-86706-167-7 (lib. bdg.)
ISBN 0-86706-166-9 (retail ed.)

Time-Life Books Inc.
is a wholly owned subsidiary of
Time Incorporated

Founder: Henry R. Luce 1898–1967
Editor-in-Chief: Henry Anatole Grunwald
President: J. Richard Munro
Chairman of the Board: Ralph P. Davidson
Executive Vice President: Clifford J. Grum
Editorial Director: Ralph Graves
Group Vice President, Books: Joan D. Manley

Time-Life Books Inc.

Editor: George Constable
Executive Editor: George Daniels
Director of Design: Louis Klein
Board of Editors: Dale M. Brown, Thomas A.
Lewis, Robert G. Mason, Ellen Phillips,
Gerry Schremp, Gerald Simons, Rosalind
Stubenberg, Kit van Tulleken
Director of Administration: David L. Harrison
Director of Research: Carolyn L. Sackett
Director of Photography: John Conrad Weiser

President: Reginald K. Brack Jr.
Senior Vice President: William Henry
Vice Presidents: George Artandi, Stephen L.
Bair, Peter G. Barnes, Robert A. Ellis,
Juanita T. James, Christopher T. Linen,
James L. Mercer, Joanne A. Pello,
Paul R. Stewart

Editorial Operations
Design: Anne B. Landry (art coordinator);
James J. Cox (quality control)
Research: Phyllis K. Wise (assistant director),
Louise D. Forstall
Copy Room: Diane Ullius (director),
Celia Beattie
Production: Gordon E. Buck,
Peter Inchauteguiz
Correspondent: Miriam Hsia (New York)

SERIES CONSULTANT
Margaret E. Happel is the author of *Ladies Home Journal Adventures in Cooking*, *Ladies Home Journal Handbook of Holiday Cuisine*, and other best-selling cookbooks, as well as the translator and adapter of Rebecca Hsu Hiu Min's *Delights of Chinese Cooking*. A food consultant based in New York City, she has been director of the food department of *Good Housekeeping* and editor of *American Home* magazine.

WINE CONSULTANT
Tom Maresca combines a full-time career teaching English literature with writing about and consuming fine wines. He is now at work on *The Wine Case Book*, which explains the techniques of wine tasting.

Cover: Richard Sax's leek and mushroom tart with ham and cheese, and a mixed vegetable slaw. See pages 78–79.

Great Meals
IN MINUTES
VEGETABLE
MENUS

TIME-LIFE BOOKS, ALEXANDRIA, VIRGINIA

Contents

MEET THE COOKS   4

VEGETABLE MENUS IN MINUTES   7

PANTRY (for this volume)   14

EQUIPMENT   16

MADHUR JAFFREY   18

Rice Pilaf with Black-Eyed Peas and Green Beans
Eggplant in Spicy Tomato Sauce   20

Persian-Style Rice with Lima Beans and Dill
Cauliflower with Garlic and Sesame Seeds / Yogurt with Tomato and Cucumber   22

Brown Rice with Mushrooms
Peas and Tomatoes with Cumin Seeds / Yogurt with Mint   24

MARLENE SOROSKY   26

Chicken in Parchment with Mushrooms and Tomatoes
Green Salad with Fried Goat Cheese   28

Deep-Dish Vegetable Pot Pies
Fresh Orange and Green Salad   30

Spaghetti Squash with Garden Vegetable Sauce
Almond Popovers with Amaretto Butter   33

BEVERLY COX   36

Eggplant Pie / Green Bean and Onion Salad
Oranges with Cinnamon   38

Louisiana-Style Mirlitons Stuffed with Ham and Shrimp
Marinated Carrots   40

Chicken Breasts with a Bouquet of Vegetables and Sweet-and-Sour Sauce
Green Salad with Herbed Vinaigrette   42

JANE SALZFASS FREIMAN   46

Seafood Salad
Cheese and Scallion Enchiladas with Guacamole Sauce   48

Watercress Soup / Broiled Scrod with Red-Pepper Sauce
Steamed New Potatoes   50

Pasta with Fresh Mushroom Sauce
Boston Lettuce, Fennel, and Radicchio Salad   52

MARTHA ROSE SHULMAN   54

Saffron Millet / Stir-Fried Tofu with Snow Peas
Hot-and-Sour Cucumber Salad   56

Chilies con Queso (Chilies with Cheese Fondue)
Spanish Rice / Guacamole Chalupas   58

Puffed Broccoli Omelets
Wild Rice with Almonds / Curried Pumpkin Purée   61

PETER KUMP   64

Fresh Beet Salad / Tomato and Onion Salad / Carrot and Horseradish Salad
Turkey Scallops with Brown Butter and Caper Sauce / Green Beans with Sweet-and-Sour Sauce   66

Celeriac Winter Salad / Chicken Piccata
Braised Fresh Spinach and Mushrooms   68

Cream of Lemon Soup / Fillets of Sole with Zucchini and Peppers
Blueberry Cream-Cheese Parfaits   71

RICHARD SAX   74

Hearty Vegetable Chowder
Herbed Buttermilk Biscuits / Tossed Green Salad   76

Leek and Mushroom Tart / Mixed Vegetable Slaw   78

Individual Pumpkin Soufflés / Oven-Roasted Chicken Breasts
Rice Pilaf with Fresh Vegetables   80

JEAN GRASSO FITZPATRICK   82

California Gazpacho
Artichoke Frittata / Roasted Peppers   84

Broiled Mushroom Caps
Risotto with Zucchini / Avocado and Red Pepper Salad   86

Penne with Broccoli Rabe
Stuffed Eggplant with Tomato Sauce / Fennel and Olive Salad   88

BARBARA TROPP   90

Savory Tofu Stew
Stir-Fried Rice with Bell Peppers and Almonds   92

Pot-Browned "Noodle Pillow" / Stir-Fried Curried Pork with Onions
Hot-and-Sour Hunan-Style Vegetables   94

Wine "Explosion" Mushroom Soup with Sweet Peas
"Old Egg" with Scallions and Shrimp / Stir-Fried Velvet Spinach with Glass Noodles   98

ACKNOWLEDGMENTS 101   INDEX 101

Meet the Cooks

MADHUR JAFFREY

Madhur Jaffrey, born in Delhi, India, came to America as an actress and then became a writer and cooking teacher. She has written for numerous national magazines, including *Gourmet*, *Bon Appetit*, and *Travel and Leisure*. She is the author of *An Invitation to Indian Cooking* and *Madhur Jaffrey's World-of-the-East Vegetarian Cooking*, winner of a Tastemaker Award. Her third cookbook, based on a BBC television series, is *Madhur Jaffrey's Indian Cooking*.

MARLENE SOROSKY

Born and raised in Oregon, Marlene Sorosky studied classical cooking in France, and then continued her culinary education in the United States with a number of noted professional chefs. She is a founder and past secretary-treasurer of the International Association of Cooking Schools and contributing editor to "The Pleasures of Cooking" magazine. Now living in California, she is the author of *Cookery for Entertaining* and *Marlene Sorosky's Year Round Holiday Cookbook*.

BEVERLY COX

Beverly Cox holds the Diplome d'Excellence from Maxim's in Paris, and the Grand Diplome from the Cordon Bleu. As a food stylist, she develops recipes for clients, and is Food Editor and Director of Food Styling for *The Cook's Magazine*. Now living in Connecticut, Beverly Cox is the author of *Gourmet Minceur*, *Minceur Italienne*, and the co-author, with Joan Whitman, of *Cooking Techniques*.

JANE SALZFASS FREIMAN

Jane Salzfass Freiman, a Chicago-based cooking instructor for several years, holds a diploma in French culinary arts from Luberon College, in Avignon, France. She has traveled extensively in Italy and is a specialist in Italian cooking. A food writer, she has a syndicated newspaper column on food processor cooking and is the author of *The Art of Food Processor Cooking*, published in 1980, which received a Tastemaker runner-up award.

MARTHA ROSE SHULMAN

Born in Connecticut, Martha Rose Shulman, daughter of writer Max Shulman, learned to appreciate many different ethnic foods as a child. She began to cook as a teenager and after college became a professional cook and food writer. She is the author of *The Vegetarian Feast*, which won a Tastemaker Award, and *Fast Vegetarian Feasts*. She now lives in Paris, where she caters and works as a private cook.

PETER KUMP

While he was a college student in Northern California, Peter Kump developed a love of cooking and subsequently studied with many prominent cooking teachers. After moving to New York, he founded the New York Cooking School, which now operates out of two New York City locations. He appears on several national television cooking programs, including "Daytime" and "Woman's Day." Peter Kump is the author of *Quiche and Pâté*.

RICHARD SAX

Food journalist and cooking instructor Richard Sax, who lives in New York City, was trained in Paris at the Cordon Bleu, and in New York. Formerly a professional chef, chef-director of the test kitchen at *Food & Wine* magazine, and consultant to Time-Life's *The Good Cook* series, he writes a monthly book review column for *Cuisine* magazine, and contributes food articles to various national publications. His latest book is *Old Fashioned Desserts*.

JEAN GRASSO FITZPATRICK

Jean Grasso Fitzpatrick, former food columnist for the magazine *Attenzione*, became interested in Italian food while doing graduate work in Italian literature. She developed a flair for cooking with vegetables after her husband became a vegetarian. A free-lance writer who lives in Ossining, New York, she has contributed numerous non-food articles to major magazines, and currently is working on an Italian cookbook.

BARBARA TROPP

Barbara Tropp, who reads and speaks fluent Mandarin, is a scholar turned Chinese cook. After studying Chinese art and literature at Princeton University, she lived for two years in Taiwan, where she learned to appreciate Chinese cooking. She returned home to New Jersey and became a practitioner and teacher of the art. She is the author of the highly acclaimed *The Modern Art of Chinese Cooking*. Now she is opening her own restaurant in San Francisco.

Vegetable Menus in Minutes

GREAT MEALS FOR FOUR, IN AN HOUR OR LESS

More than other foods, vegetables offer limitless variations in texture, taste, and color. Most—especially the leafy green ones—are good raw, but you can cook them, too, using almost any technique: boiling, steaming, sautéing, stir frying, deep frying, grilling, baking, or broiling.

Vegetables are any edible portion of any plant with soft green stems. They are classified according to what part of the plant is edible: roots and tubers (beets and potatoes); bulbs (the onion family); stems (asparagus and kohlrabi); leaves (lettuces and spinach); leafstalks (celery, rhubarb, and fennel); immature flowers (broccoli and cauliflower); seeds and seed pods (dried mature legumes and fresh young peas and beans). Another category is fruit-vegetables. Botanically, these are fruits because they contain one or more seeds surrounded by the flesh of the plant; but for purposes of cooking and eating, they qualify as vegetables because they are not as sweet as fruits and usually are not eaten out of the hand. This group includes tomatoes, green peppers, eggplant, avocados, corn, squash, and cucumbers. Mushrooms, too, are treated as vegetables although they really are fungi, those flowerless, rootless parasites that live on other plants.

Most of the vegetables we eat today are the domesticated descendants of ancient wild plants. Formal vegetable cultivation—the first taming of wild plants for a predictable harvest—probably dates back to at least 8000 B.C., when farmers in the Middle East began to cultivate certain legumes. According to other evidence, Southeast Asian farmers may have cultivated crops as early as 9750 B.C. But wherever it occurred, the domestication of vegetables was an important step from nomadic life to civilization as we now define it. Archeological records show that ancient Egyptians grew asparagus, cabbage, cucumbers, and lettuce; Egyptian tomb drawings depict laborers eating onions. By the first century A.D., Roman farmers were harvesting diverse crops, and vegetables had become a popular Roman food. The oldest surviving Western cookbook, written by a Roman epicure 1900 years ago, features vegetable recipes along with some tips, such as advising cooks to boil green vegetables with baking soda to retain the green color, a practice today's nutritionists would dis-

courage, since baking soda destroys vitamin C and turns vegetables bitter.

An astonishing variety of vegetables grew in the Americas, types that until the early sixteenth century had been unknown to Europeans, Africans, and Asians: peanuts, vanilla beans, tomatoes, pineapples, green beans, lima beans, sweet peppers, potatoes, chilies, and corn. The discovery of the New World meant a new dietary world. Peruvian Indians had cultivated the white potato for many centuries before the Spanish conquered South America and took the potato to Spain. It became a staple all over Europe, especially in Germany, France, and Ireland. Tomatoes, another South American vegetable, were cultivated in Morocco by the Spaniards who brought them from South America; but Europe was slow to believe that tomatoes were edible. In the sixteenth and seventeenth centuries, as explorers and settlers traversed the globe, they carried seeds, roots, and cuttings back and forth between the Old and New Worlds, a crisscrossing vegetable traffic that led to the universal cultivation and use of a wide range of vegetables.

During the colonial period, Americans enjoyed a great variety of fresh vegetables in season, native crops as well as varieties that colonists had imported from Europe. Thomas Jefferson's *Garden Book* of 1774 and his notes about shipments into the Washington, D.C., market during his presidency clearly document the availability of fresh asparagus, broccoli, corn, lettuces, and herbs, along with dozens of other seasonal vegetables. Books such as *American Cookery* by Amelia Simmons, published in 1796, provide evidence that these vegetables were cooked with care, for the author advises cooks to boil green beans and asparagus quickly to prevent loss of color. A century or so later, however, many Americans routinely served vegetables only as side dishes (often overcooked and unseasoned) to the meat main course. Thus it is not surprising that generations of Americans have not appreciated their own native crops.

Crop planting and cultivation were often casual, even primitive, until twentieth-century scientists and farmers developed breeding systems for producing fast-growing, disease-resistant, and very prolific plants. Only since the turn of the century have new ways of processing revolutionized the availability of vegetables. Canned vegetables, which came into increasing use in the decades after the Civil War, gave consumers a year-round harvest, but flash-frozen vegetables, widely marketed after World War

A display of fresh vegetables, opposite, in brilliant colors and beautiful shapes includes samples of almost every vegetable category: red cabbage and parsley; tomatoes, okra, corn, avocados, squash; rhubarb; ginger and radishes; onions and garlic; artichokes; and peas.

II, better captured the flavor of garden-fresh vegetables.

Today, Americans' attitudes towards eating vegetables have changed. They have rediscovered the joys of fresh vegetables and the value of fresh produce as an essential element in fine cooking as well as good nutrition. Imaginative salads—a spectrum of raw vegetables and lettuces, creatively combined—are replacing the standard offering of a chunk of iceberg lettuce and a slice of tomato. Good supermarkets and restaurants now offer an improved repertoire of vegetables—new kinds of squashes and peas, sweet peppers in a choice of colors and types, eggplants in several varieties, and newcomers such as celeriac.

Good health is another compelling reason for this vegetable revival. Vegetables contain essential vitamins, minerals, carbohydrates, and fiber bulk. Some, such as the legumes, are also high in protein. Furthermore, in 1982 the National Academy of Sciences reported that the consumption of carotene-rich (carotenes are the carriers of vitamin A) dark-green or yellow vegetables, such as spinach and carrots, and cruciferous vegetables, such as broccoli, cabbage, cauliflower, and brussels sprouts, is associated with a lower risk of certain cancers. And though ours is traditionally a meat-eating culture, some Americans, for reasons of health or philosophy, have always been vegetarians, avoiding animal protein altogether (or almost so), as the vegetarians of Asia and the Middle East also do. But whatever the reason—culinary, nutritional, or philosophical—a vegetable revolution is taking place in America. Americans are not only eating larger amounts of fresh vegetables, but they are also demanding more and better produce and are taking greater pride in their vegetable recipes.

On the following pages, nine of America's most talented cooks present 27 complete menus featuring vegetables and vegetable-based meals. Although 15 menus *are* vegetarian, this is not a vegetarian cookbook. You will find meats and cheeses as well as pasta along with the vegetables, but in every menu the emphasis is on the vegetables. Every menu can be made in an hour or less, and the cooks focus on a new kind of American cuisine that borrows ideas and techniques from around the world but values our native traditions, too. They use fresh produce—no canned vegetables or powdered sauces or other questionable shortcuts. The other ingredients (vinegars, spices, herbs, etc.) are all high quality yet available, for the most part, in supermarkets—or occasionally in a specialty shop. Each of the menus serves four people and includes other dishes that work perfectly with the vegetables.

The color photographs accompanying each meal show exactly how the dishes will look when you take them to the table. The cooks and the test kitchen have planned the meals for good appearance as well as good taste—the vegetables are brilliant and fresh, the color combinations appetizing. The table settings feature bright colors, simple flower arrangements, and attractive if not necessarily expensive serving pieces. You can readily adapt your own tableware to these menus in convenient ways that will please you and your guests.

For each menu, the Editors, with advice from the cooks, suggest wines and other beverages to accompany the meals. And there are suggestions for the best uses of leftovers and for appropriate desserts. On each recipe page, too, you will find a range of other tips—from the best way to peel and seed a tomato to tricks for selecting the freshest produce. All the recipes have been tested meticulously, both for taste and appearance—and to make sure that even a relatively inexperienced cook can do them within the time limit.

BEFORE YOU START
Great Meals in Minutes is designed for efficiency and ease. The books will work best for you when you follow these suggestions:

1. Read the rules (pages 8–10) for selecting and storing fresh vegetables, keeping the seasonal availability of certain vegetables in mind.

2. Refresh yourself on the few simple cooking techniques on the following pages. They will quickly become second nature and will help you produce professional meals in minutes.

3. Read the menus *before* you shop. Each one opens with a list of all the required ingredients. Check for those few you need to buy; most items will already be on your pantry shelf.

4. Check the equipment list on page 16. A good, sharp knife—or knives—and pots and pans of the right shape and material are essential for making great meals in minutes. This may be the time to look critically at what you own and to plan to pick up a few things. The right equipment can turn cooking from a chore into a creative experience.

5. Get out everything you need before you start to cook: the lists at the beginning of each menu tell just what is required. To save steps, keep your ingredients close at hand and always put them in the same place, so you can reach for them instinctively.

6. Take your ingredients from the refrigerator early enough for them to come to room temperature so as to cut cooking time. Make sure that all vegetables are cleaned ahead of time and are ready for preparation.

7. Follow the step-by-step game plan with each menu. That way, you can be sure of having the entire meal ready to serve at the right moment.

SELECTING AND STORING VEGETABLES
Vegetable quality is never guaranteed. Climate, soil, and sunshine affect vegetables as much as the care they get during harvesting, packing, and shipping. Also, the time lapse between picking and cooking affects appearance, taste, and nutritive value. Vegetables start to deteriorate as soon as they are picked. The best advice, therefore, is to buy produce locally during its natural growing season either from a farmers' market or from a greengrocer supplied by local farmers. When you shop at the supermarket, remember that markets vary in the selection and handling of fresh produce. Find one that offers seasonal and local items, then shop carefully, examining produce

for any signs of age or decay. Buy only crisp, firm, fresh-looking vegetables.

Canned or frozen vegetables are rarely as good as fresh-picked. If the vegetable you want is out of season, try to find another with similar taste and texture. The directions accompanying each menu in this book usually include suggestions for substitutions. In some cases, canned or frozen vegetables are acceptable alternatives: canned tomatoes are as good as fresh for soups and sauces, and some frozen vegetables—for instance, black-eyed peas, lima beans, artichoke hearts, baby corn, spinach, and green peas—are good alternatives provided you do not overcook them.

Most growers wax vegetables to restore the natural sheen scrubbed off in a general cleaning process after harvest. This edible wax coating brightens vegetables, adds eye appeal, and retards decay by sealing in natural moisture and nutrients. Vegetables should be rinsed, of course, but there is no need to wash off this wax.

Roots and tubers: This category includes potatoes, beets, ginger, Jerusalem artichokes, carrots, radishes, sweet potatoes, turnips, and celeriac. The cooking method dictates the type of potato you buy. There are two basic types: waxy (low starch)—long white, round white, round red, and all new potatoes; and nonwaxy (high starch)—long ovals with rough skins. To quickly determine potato type, slice a raw potato in two and rub the cut halves together. Starchy potato halves stick together, but low-starch halves do not. Waxy potatoes are best boiled or steamed. Nonwaxy potatoes are most desirable for baking, pan roasting, and mashing; they are ideal for French fries. All potatoes should be firm, without sprouts or green bitter-tasting spots.

Do not wash roots and tubers before storing. Cut off any green tops; they draw moisture from the vegetable. Wrap all roots and tubers in plastic bags and store in the refrigerator. Potatoes, sweet potatoes, and rutabagas are exceptions. These should be kept in a cool, dark, dry spot. At room temperature, they last for one week; at 50 degrees F., they keep up to two months.

Bulbs: The allium—onion, garlic, etc.—family functions both as seasonings and as vegetables. Onions come in a considerable range: chive, scallion, pearl, creole, Bermuda, leek, white boiling, shallot, and yellow globe. Mildly oniony chives (green shoots picked before a bulb forms) make tender garnishes; baby pearl onions are delicious pickled; the versatile yellow globe onion is a kitchen staple.

Onions should be firm and well shaped. Old onions will have green sprouts and feel soggy. Scallions, leeks, chives, and shallots, stored in a plastic bag in the refrigerator, will last for several days. All other onions with papery skins must remain cool and dry. They will deteriorate quickly in the dampness of the refrigerator, so store them in their mesh bags in a cool, dry, dark place away from direct light, which turns them green and bitter. Never store onions near potatoes. The moisture they absorb from potatoes causes onions to decay. Garlic keeps best at room tempera-ture in wire baskets in a cool, dry, dark place or in special lidded pottery crocks that have ventilation holes.

Stems: Asparagus, the welcome harbinger of spring, comes in two different types: green and white. The familiar green spears are readily available in most markets, but the white ones are sold fresh only in select greengrocers or, more commonly, packaged in glass jars. Select spears that are straight, with compact pointed tips, and that are crisp rather than spongy. Slightly limp spears firm up when soaked in cold water. Asparagus is highly perishable, so it must be kept in the coldest part of the refrigerator. Wrap stem ends in dampened paper towels and place whole spears in a perforated plastic bag. (For fennel and *bok choy*, sometimes also classed as stems, see *Leafstalks*, below.)

Leaves: Leafy greens—spinach, cabbage, lettuce, endive, kale, broccoli rabe, sorrel, and mustard greens—generally are available all year. The best tasting leafy vegetables are young, with bright crisp leaves and no bruises, yellowing spots, or wilt. Sort through loose leaves right away to detect any spoilage. Highly perishable, leafy vegetables need storage in the coldest part of the refrigerator. Except for lettuce, wrap them, unwashed, in a perforated plastic bag. Rinsed and completely drained lettuce, wrapped in a kitchen towel and then a plastic bag, stays crisp for several days and is salad-ready.

Leafstalks: These textured firm vegetables are erect stems with leafy tops; the category includes rhubarb, celery, fennel, Swiss chard, and *bok choy*. Tender young stalks are firm and unblemished; tough older stalks are coarse and pithy. Yellowed leaves or leaves with mushy brown spots indicate that the vegetable is old or has been overchilled, and has thus become tasteless. Leafy stalks, with all limp outer leaves removed, need refrigeration. Wrap unwashed stalks in a plastic bag—depending on the variety, they last up to one week.

Immature flowers: Artichokes, broccoli, and cauliflower belong to this group. All have immature flower heads or clusters of heads surrounded by leaves and set on thick fleshy stalks. The globe artichoke, the unopened flower of a thistle, looks like a green-leafed crown circling a prickly choke and a saucer-shaped bottom. Artichokes with compact, hefty heads and firm green leaves are the ones to buy. Store them, unwashed, wrapped in a plastic bag, in the refrigerator. They keep four to five days.

Fresh broccoli and its first cousin, cauliflower, have firm stalks and compact flowered heads. Broccoli should be dark green, and cauliflower should be white without any dark speckles. Neither should have any sign of yellowing. Both need thorough rinsing before storage. Store them in plastic bags in the coldest part of your refrigerator. They keep well for three to five days.

Seeds and seed pods: This broad category encompasses seeds, peas, or beans in pods such as snow peas, and young shoots such as bean sprouts. Choose the smallest and youngest peas, with pods that are wrinkle free, moist, and firm. Dried legumes are the mature seeds of plants with

Cooking at high temperatures can be dangerous, but not if you follow a few simple tips:

▶ Water added to hot fat will always cause spattering. Take time, therefore, to dry foods thoroughly on cloth or paper towel before you add them to sauté pan or frying oil.

▶ Lay the food in the pan gently. Otherwise the fat will certainly spatter.

▶ Be aware of your cooking environment. If you are boiling or steaming some foods while sautéing others,

place the pots far enough apart so the water is unlikely to splash into the oil.

▶ Remember that alcohol—wine, brandy, or spirits—may occasionally catch fire when you add it to a very hot pan. If this happens, stand back for your own protection, and then quickly cover the pan with a lid. The fire will instantly subside.

▶ Keep pot holders and mitts close enough to be handy, but never hang them above the burners—nor should you lay them on the stove top.

---

pods, dried either before or after being shelled. These are available in boxes or plastic bags at most supermarkets or health food shops. Although they have a long shelf life if stored closed in an airtight container, you should not use any that are more than a year old because they darken and harden with age and may disintegrate during cooking. Notice the date on the box and, if you store dried legumes in a glass container, jot the purchase date on a piece of masking tape and stick it on the jar lid.

Fruit-vegetables: This category includes tomatoes, avocados, sweet peppers, eggplant, corn, squash, and cucumbers—warm-weather plants that are really fruits. Fruit-vegetables taste best when allowed to vine ripen; because they are delicate, plan to use them a day or two after purchase.

Out-of-season tomatoes must be picked hard and green for long-distance shipping, then artificially ripened. Your best bet are those labeled "hothouse" because these are picked almost fully ripe, carefully packed in sturdy crates, then shipped to local markets. A tip for ripening hothouse tomatoes: buy them several days before you plan to use them, and put them in a loosely closed paper bag with an apple. Unless tomatoes are on the verge of decay, never refrigerate them because this mars their full flavor.

Ripe avocados are slightly soft to the touch, with no bruises or dark spots. An underripe avocado ripens easily, within a day or two, if you wrap it in a brown paper bag and leave it at room temperature. To test for ripeness, stick a toothpick in at the stem end. If the toothpick goes in and out easily, the avocado is perfectly ripe. Ripe avocados, stored in the refrigerator, keep for three to five days.

Sweet peppers should be firm, brightly colored, and well shaped. Wrapped in a plastic bag, they last for a week in the refrigerator. Eggplant, bought firm, bright, and shiny, with fresh green caps, need refrigeration to retain moisture. Store them unwashed in a plastic bag. Zucchini, yellow crookneck, pattypan, and all summer squash should look fresh, feel firm, and have tender skin. Stored in a plastic bag in the refrigerator, they last for up to one week. Treat cucumbers, a relative of these squash, the same way. Winter squash—pumpkin, butternut, acorn, hubbard, and chayote—should have hard rinds and feel hefty. These keep for several months in a cool, dry place.

As any enthusiast will report, fresh sweet corn tastes best picked from the stalk, then immediately shucked and popped into a pot of boiling unsalted water. Most cooks obviously cannot follow such a plan. So, select ears with fresh green husks, plump juicy kernels, and silk that is free from decay. If you can, cook and eat the corn as soon as you buy it; otherwise, store unhusked ears in the coldest part of your refrigerator and cook them later the same day. Never leave corn out at room temperature because warm air quickly converts its sugar to starch, harming both sweetness and flavor.

Mushrooms: Fresh, standard, domestic mushrooms have tightly fitting caps that curve over the stems and cover the gills on the underside. If the caps flare open, exposing the gills, the mushrooms are old and dry. Since mushrooms are highly perishable, store them unwashed for no more than two to three days in a loosely covered container in the refrigerator. Stored too long, mushrooms become soggy and lose flavor and texture.

Barbara Tropp (pages 98–99) calls for a selection of fresh mushrooms from four unusual varieties: Japanese enokitake and shiitake, Chinese oyster, and French chanterelle. Their cap shapes and colors differ from those of the standard mushroom varieties so, when shopping, select mushrooms that feel firm and are not slimy.

Dried mushrooms, in plastic or cellophane bags, keep indefinitely on the pantry shelf.

HANDLING VEGETABLES

Preparing whole vegetables for cooking can be a satisfying experience; with proper tools, care, and precision, you can turn out beautifully cut vegetables. For cutting by hand, you need a vegetable peeler, a sharp knife, and a cutting board. A food processor is a great convenience, but most practiced cooks enjoy doing some cutting by hand, whether or not they own a food processor. Besides, the processor cannot always replace the cutting board and knife: roll cutting, for example, must be done by hand.

The vegetable type and how you plan to use it determine how you cut up a vegetable. For instance, potatoes are diced for hash browns, quartered for pan roasting, and cut into strips for French fries. Correct cutting also permits even cooking. You need to know seven basic cutting techniques to prepare vegetables: chopping, dicing, mincing, slicing, roll cutting, julienning, and shredding.

Remember that cutting vegetables, like any other technique, takes practice. Try to improve your speed and facility: an accomplished cook should be able to mince a large onion in under a minute.

Chopping, Dicing, and Mincing

These terms are used interchangeably to describe the same basic technique, the only difference being the size of the cube. Fine or coarse chopping produces small irregularly shaped pieces; dicing produces small, uniform, square cubes; mincing reduces diced vegetables to very fine pieces, just short of a purée.

To chop a vegetable, first peel it, if necessary, then put it on the cutting board and, with a sharp chef's knife, slice it to make cuts parallel to the board. (You must first slice through a round or cylindrical vegetable to create a flat surface, then turn it down on the cutting board. Otherwise you can never cut quickly and evenly.) Make a series of vertical cuts across; then, holding the vegetable together with the fingers of your other hand, rotate it a quarter turn and make another series of vertical cuts perpendicular to those. For finer chopping, push the pieces into a neat pile with the knife blade and—grasping the knife handle in one hand, holding the tip steady on the board with the other, and moving the handle only—chop the vegetable in an arc. Push the pieces together with the knife blade and start again.

The same principle applies to dicing and mincing. If you make uniform horizontal and vertical perpendicular cuts about a quarter inch apart, the pieces will fall into an even dice. To dice a whole onion, peel off the papery outer skin and, if necessary, the first tough white layer. Slice the onion in half and place flat side down on the cutting board. Slice the onion through at quarter-inch intervals lengthwise up to, but not through, its root end—this end keeps the layers together. Grasp the onion at its root end and, at quarter-inch intervals, make slices horizontal to the cutting board. Finally, in quarter-inch intervals, slice the onion through from one end to the other. This produces a uniform dice.

Slicing

Vegetable slices are flat, uniform pieces. For slicing round vegetables, cut a thin strip from one side and hold the vegetable cut side down on the board to keep it steady. Making vertical cuts, slice the vegetable to the desired thickness.

Roll Cutting

This is a special method for long cylindrical vegetables such as carrots, asparagus, or zucchini. First, peel the vegetable if the recipe so directs. Now make a sharp diagonal cut perhaps an inch from one end, at about a 45-degree angle. Then roll the vegetable a quarter turn and slice again at the same angle, about an inch from the first cut. Continue until you have sliced the whole length. Because the diagonal slices expose more of the insides of the vegetables, they will cook faster and absorb more flavor than will conventional slices.

Julienne

Julienne vegetables are cut into thin matchstick strips of uniform size, an attractive way to prepare them for garnishes or quick-cooking. To cut long vegetables such as carrots into julienne, peel them first, then cut them into two-inch lengths. Stand each length on its end and hold it firmly at the top with your fingertips. Cut down in ¼- or ⅛-inch slices and stack up two or three of these thin slices. Cut slices through into fine strips. Cut a round vegetable such as a potato or beet into ⅛-inch-thick slices. Stack the slices on each other, then cut through the stack, making strips ⅛ inch wide. These strips can be cut to any length you want.

Shredding

Shredded cabbage or lettuce is easier to work with than the whole uncut leaves. To shred, cut the lettuce or cabbage head in half. Remove the core. Then place one half with its flat side down on the cutting board. Starting at the top and cutting to the core end, make vertical slices with a sharp knife. The closer the slices, the finer the shreds.

COOKING IN LIQUIDS

Boiling and Blanching

The trick to boiling lies in timing: overboiled vegetables lose both taste and texture. When boiling whole vegetables, choose those of a uniform size, or cut them into uniform pieces.

There are two basic boiling methods: With the first method, vegetables boil in a minimal amount of water in a covered pot. This minimizes nutrient loss and maximizes flavor retention, but you must watch closely lest the water boil away and the vegetables scorch.

The second, which professional cooks often use, calls for filling a large stockpot with water and bringing the water to a rolling boil. Boil vegetables in an uncovered pot until they are tender but not soft. If drained immediately in a colander, they stop cooking. Serve them at once. Quick boiling is ideal for most green vegetables, as it retains their color. Moreover, the intense flavor of such vegetables as cabbage disperses in the water. The disadvantage is that boiling water leaches out some nutrients.

Both methods suit mild vegetables such as carrots and potatoes. Since all vegetables cook at different rates, test for doneness often. To shorten the cooking time for broccoli and asparagus, peel their tough stems; for potatoes and eggplant, peel completely.

Blanching, also called parboiling, is an invaluable technique. Immerse whole or cut vegetables for a few moments in boiling water, then "refresh" them—that is, plunge them in cold water to stop their cooking and set their colors. Blanching softens or tenderizes dense or crisp vegetables, often as a preliminary to further cooking by another method, such as stir frying.

Steaming

A fast and nutritious way to cook vegetables is to steam them on a wire rack over boiling water in a covered pot. In some respects this is the optimum cooking method: It requires no fat and preserves nutrients that otherwise might be lost in the cooking liquid. It also keeps taste, texture, and color intact. Special steaming pots come with racks and tight-fitting lids, or you can improvise your own. (See page 17 for an illustration of a collapsible vegetable steamer.) In either case, the boiling water must not touch the bottom of the rack holding the vegetables. To prevent overcooking, test vegetables as they steam; when they are crisp-tender, they are done.

Braising
Braised vegetables, cooked in butter or oil and minimal liquid in a covered pot, emerge moist and lightly browned. Root vegetables and leafy greens are particularly suited to this slow-cook method. The cooking liquid for highly seasoned vegetables is usually stock or water. Strong-tasting vegetables like brussels sprouts, fennel, celeriac, and turnips benefit from parboiling first. If you wish, you may brown vegetables before braising: this seals in flavor that otherwise would be lost in the cooking liquid. Sugar added to the braising liquid offsets the acid taste of vegetables such as tomatoes. You can braise vegetables singly or in combination with others for a blending of flavors, as Peter Kump does with fresh spinach and mushrooms (see page 70).

COOKING WITH OIL
Two methods produce very similar results, and both are ideal for cooking small vegetable pieces, slivers, cubes, or rounds.

Sautéing
Sautéing is a form of quick frying, with no lid on the pan. In French, *sauter* means "to jump," which is what vegetables or small pieces of food do when you shake the sauté pan. The purpose is to lightly brown food pieces and seal in their juices before further cooking. This technique has three critical elements: the right type of pan, the pan heated to the proper temperature, and ingredients that you have drained well or patted dry.

The sauté pan: A proper sauté pan is 10 to 12 inches in diameter and has 2- to 3-inch straight sides that allow you to turn food while keeping the fat from spattering. It has a heavy bottom that slides easily over a burner.

The best material (and the most expensive) for a sauté pan is tin-lined copper because it is a superior heat conductor. Stainless steel with a layer of aluminum or copper on the bottom is also very efficient. (Stainless steel alone is a poor conductor.) Heavy-gauge aluminum works well but will discolor acidic food such as tomatoes. Therefore, you should not use aluminum if the food is to be cooked for more than 20 minutes after the initial browning. Another option is to select a heavy-duty sauté pan made of strong, heat-conductive aluminum alloys. This type of professional cookware is smooth and stick resistant.

The ultimate test of a good sauté pan is whether or not it heats evenly: hot spots will burn the food rather than brown it. A heavy sauté pan that does not heat evenly can be saved. Rub the pan with a generous amount of vegeta-

ble oil. Then place a half inch of salt in the pan and heat it slowly over low heat, about 10 to 15 minutes, until very hot. Empty the salt, do not wash the pan, and rub it with vegetable oil again.

Select a sauté pan large enough to hold the food without crowding. The heat of the fat and air spaces around and between the pieces allow browning. Crowding results in steaming—a technique that lets the juices out rather than seals them in. If your sauté pan is too small to prevent crowding, sauté in batches or use two pans at once.

You will find sauté pans for sale without lids, but be sure you buy one with a tight-fitting cover. Many recipes call for sautéing first, then lowering the heat and cooking the food, covered, for an additional 10 to 20 minutes. Make sure the handle is long and comfortable to hold.

When you have finished sautéing, never immerse the hot pan in cold water—this will warp the metal. Let the pan cool slightly, then add water, and let it sit until you are ready to wash it.

Use a wooden spatula or tongs to keep the food moving in the pan as you shake it over the burner. If the meat sticks—as it occasionally will—a metal turner will loosen it best. Turn the pieces so that all surfaces come into contact with the hot oil and none of them sticks. Do not use a fork—particularly not with meats.

The fat: A combination of half butter and half vegetable or peanut oil is perfect for most sautéing: it heats to high temperatures without burning and allows you to have a rich butter flavor at the same time. Always use unsalted butter for cooking: it tastes better and will not add unwanted salt to your recipe. Butter alone makes a wonderful-tasting sauté; but butter, whether salted or unsalted, burns at a high temperature. If you prefer an all-butter flavor, clarify the butter before you begin. This means removing the milky residue, which is the part that scorches. To clarify, heat the butter in a small saucepan over medium heat and, using a cooking spoon, skim off the foam as it rises to the top, and discard it. Keep skimming until no more foam appears. Pour off the remaining oil, making sure to leave the milky residue at the bottom of the pan. The oil is clarified butter; use this for sautés. Ideally, you should clarify butter a batch at a time. But it is a simple matter to make a large quantity of it and store it in your refrigerator; it will keep for two to three weeks. Watch carefully when you sauté in olive oil; discard any scorched oil and start with fresh if necessary. If you allow the pan to cool slightly, you can wipe up the oil with a paper towel wrapped around the end of a wooden spoon.

To sauté properly, heat the sauté fat until it is hot but not smoking. When you see small bubbles on top of the fat, it is almost hot enough to smoke. In that case, lower the heat. When using butter and oil together, add the butter to the hot oil. After the foam from the melting butter subsides, you are ready to sauté. If the temperature is just right, the food will sizzle when you put it in.

Stir Frying
Basic to Chinese cuisine, this fast-cook method requires very little oil, and the foods—which you stir continu-

Making Stock

Although canned chicken broth or stock is all right for emergencies, homemade chicken stock has a rich flavor that is hard to match. Moreover, the commercial broths—particularly the canned ones—are likely to be oversalted.

To make your own broth, save chicken parts as they accumulate and put them in a bag in the freezer; then have a rainy-day stock-making session using one of the recipes below. The skin from a yellow onion will add color; the optional veal bone will add extra flavor and richness to the stock.

3 pounds bony chicken parts, such as wings, back, and neck
1 veal knuckle (optional)
3 quarts cold water
1 yellow unpeeled onion, stuck with 2 cloves
2 stalks celery with leaves, cut in 2
12 crushed peppercorns
2 carrots, scraped and cut into 2-inch lengths
4 sprigs parsley
1 bay leaf
1 tablespoon fresh thyme, or 1 teaspoon dried
Salt (optional)

1. Wash chicken parts and veal knuckle (if you are using it) and drain. Place in large soup kettle or stockpot (any big pot) with the remaining ingredients—except salt. Cover pot and bring to a boil over moderate heat.

2. Lower heat and simmer broth, partly covered, 2 to 3 hours. Skim foam and scum from top of broth several times. Add salt to taste after broth has cooked 1 hour.

3. Strain broth through fine sieve placed over large bowl. Discard chicken pieces, vegetables, and seasonings. Let broth cool uncovered (this will speed cooling process). When completely cool, refrigerate. Fat will rise and congeal conveniently at top. You may skim it off and discard it or leave it as protective covering for broth.

For many of the meals in this volume, you may prefer to use vegetable rather than chicken stock, particularly when you want to intensify the vegetable flavor of a recipe. A properly prepared vegetable stock, made from an assortment of fresh vegetables, is a flavorful base for a variety of soups, stews, or braised vegetable dishes. Unlike meat stocks, a vegetable stock cooks quickly because there are no bones to simmer or

fat to skim off. For a richly flavored stock, vary the types of vegetables you use: carrots, cabbage, and parsnips are sweet; leeks, celery, turnips, and onions are aromatic. Wash all vegetables, and peel them when necessary. To cook the vegetables quickly and to draw out the maximum amount of flavor, coarsely chop them either by hand or in a blender or food processor. To add extra flavor to the stock, you can include bay leaves, peppercorns, parsley, and garlic, as well as an assortment of herbs, such as a pinch of thyme, basil, or tarragon.

Vegetable Stock

2 leeks, white part only
3 carrots
2 celery stalks
2 to 3 yellow onions
3 to 4 cloves garlic
1 turnip (optional)
1 parsnip (optional)
6 parsley sprigs
1 bay leaf
1 teaspoon salt
6 peppercorns
½ teaspoon dried thyme, tarragon, or basil

1. Trim leeks of roots and green tops. Make 2 lengthwise cuts down through bulb to within ½ inch of root end. Spread apart and wash carefully under cold running water to remove sand. Drain and chop coarsely. Place in large soup kettle or stockpot.

2. Strip celery of leaves and reserve. Peel celery and carrots. Chop coarsely and add to stockpot with the celery leaves.

3. Peel and quarter onions; reserve skins. Peel garlic cloves and add to pot with onions. Add onion skins, if desired, to give stock a natural golden color.

4. If using turnip or parsnip, peel, chop, and add to pot.

5. Add herbs and spices and cold water to cover, approximately 1½ quarts. Cover pot and bring to a boil over medium heat.

6. Lower heat and simmer, partly covered, approximately 1 hour.

7. Strain and chill if not using immediately.

---

ously—fry quickly over a very high heat. This is ideal for cooking bite-size shredded or thinly sliced portions of vegetables, fish, meat, or poultry alone or in combination. Barbara Tropp (page 97) stir fries cauliflower flowerets, carrot rounds, and sliced zucchini for a dish of hot-and-sour vegetables.

OVEN COOKING

Broiling
In broiling, the food cooks directly under the source of the heat. To ensure that the interior is done before the exterior burns, move the broiling rack five to six inches from the heat source. Because vegetables contain no oil or fat, they will burn unless you brush them with a coating of oil

or butter—this browns the exterior while it keeps the interior fresh tasting. Madhur Jaffrey broils eggplant slices (page 21) before topping them with a spicy tomato sauce, and Jean Grasso Fitzpatrick (page 87) broils mushroom caps.

Baking
A simple dry-heat method to cook whole vegetables or mixed-vegetable casseroles, baking also serves as an alternate to boiling vegetables you plan to purée and season. You can bake vegetables with seasonings, sauces, and savory ingredients, or you can split vegetables and stuff them with a filling, as Beverly Cox does (page 41), as another successful baking method for vegetables.

Pantry (for this volume)

A well-stocked, properly organized pantry is a time-saver for anyone who wants to prepare great meals in the shortest time possible. Location is the critical factor for staple storage. Whether your pantry consists of a small refrigerator and two or three shelves over the sink or a large freezer-refrigerator and whole room just off the kitchen, you must protect staples from heat and light.

In maintaining or restocking your pantry, follow these rules:

1. Store staples by kind and date. Canned goods need a separate shelf or a separate spot on the shelf. Put the oldest cans in front, so that you need not examine each one as you pull it out. Keep track of refrigerated and frozen staples by jotting the date on the package or writing it on a bit of masking tape.

2. Store flour, sugar, and other dry ingredients in canisters or jars with tight lids, where they will last for months. Glass and clear plastic allow you to see at a glance how much remains.

3. Keep a running grocery list near where you cook so that when a staple such as olive oil, sugar, or flour is half gone, you will be sure to stock up.

ON THE SHELF:

Almond extract

Bread

Capers, bottled

Capers are usually packed in vinegar (and less frequently in salt). If you use those bottled in vinegar, rinse them under cold water before using them.

Chocolate (unsweetened)

Cornstarch or arrowroot

Curry paste

Flour

All-purpose (ground for any use from cakes to bread), bleached, or unbleached.

Herbs and spices

Fresh herbs are always best; the flavor is much better than in dried herbs. Many fresh herbs are now available at produce markets. If you like, you can grow basil, chervil, oregano, sage, and—depending on climate—several other herbs in a small garden outdoors or on a sunny windowsill. Fresh herbs should be used immediately. The following herbs and spices, however, are perfectly acceptable in dried or packaged form—but buy in small amounts and use as quickly as possible. In measuring herbs, remember that three parts of fresh herbs will equal one part dried. *Note:* Dried chives and parsley should not be on your shelf, since they have little or no flavor. But freeze-dried chives are acceptable.

allspice
basil
bay leaves
cinnamon (ground)
cloves (whole)
coriander (ground)
cumin (whole and ground)
curry powder
fennel (whole)
fines herbes
ginger (ground)
mustard (dry)
nutmeg
oregano
pepper
> *black, whole peppercorns*
> These are ripe peppercorns dried in their black skins. Grind with a pepper mill.
> *Cayenne pepper*
> *red pepper flakes*
> Also called crushed red pepper.
> *white, whole peppercorns*
> These are like the black variety but are dried without the dark skin. Use them in pale sauces when black pepper specks would spoil the appearance.

saffron (threads)
> Made from the dried stamens of a species of crocus, this expensive seasoning adds both color and flavor.

salt
> Use coarse—also known as Kosher—salt because of its superior flavor and coarse texture. It is pure salt with no additives. Kosher salt tastes saltier than table salt. When the recipe calls for Kosher salt, you can substitute in the following proportion: ¾ teaspoon Kosher salt equals 1 teaspoon table salt.

tarragon
thyme
turmeric (ground)

Honey

Horseradish root

Hot pepper sauce

Jalapeño peppers

Maple syrup

Mushrooms (dried)

Nuts

almonds

Oils

peanut or vegetable
> Because these neutral oils add little or no taste to the food and have high smoking points, they are good for sautéing.

olive oil
> Sample French, Greek, Spanish, and Italian oils (Luccan oil, from the Tuscan region, is sure to be in your supermarket) until you find the taste you like best. Each has its own flavor. Buy only virgin or first-pressing oil; the oil from the second pressing is full of fruit pulp that burns at high heat. Good olive oils may vary in color from green to golden yellow.

safflower oil
> A polyunsaturated oil, especially favored by those on a low-cholesterol diet.

sesame oil (Chinese and Japanese)
> Used as a seasoning in Oriental cooking and sold in the Oriental section of most supermarkets. Keeps indefinitely when refrigerated.

Onions
> Store all dry-skinned onions in a cool, dry place.

garlic
> The most pungent of the onion family. Garlic powder and garlic salt are no substitute for the real thing.

leeks
> Subtle onion flavor, used for soups and in sautés. Store leeks in the refrigerator.

scallions
> Also called green onions. Mild flavor. Use the white bulbs as well as the fresh green tops. Wrap in plastic and store in the refrigerator, or chop coarsely, wrap in plastic, and freeze.

shallots
> A sweet and delicate cross between onions and garlic. Use chopped for best flavor. Buy the largest you can find because they are easier to peel and chop.

white onions
yellow onions
> The all-purpose cooking onion; strong flavor—good for flavoring stock.

Pasta and noodles, dried or fresh

Italian
> *fettuccine*
> *linguine*
> *penne*
> *ziti*

Oriental
> *bean threads,*
> *Chinese egg noodles*

Pumpkin, canned
Rice
long-grain
    Lighter and fluffier than
    short-grain when cooked.
medium-grain
short-grain (arborio)
wild rice

Seeds
poppy
sesame
sunflower

Soy sauce

Sugar
brown sugar
confectioners' sugar
granulated sugar

Tomatoes
peeled Italian plum tomatoes
    For tomato sauces, canned
    plum tomatoes are an ac-
    ceptable substitute for ripe
    tomatoes.
tomatoes in purée
tomato juice
tomato paste
    Also for sauces. With
    canned paste, spoon out un-
    used portions in 1-table-
    spoon amounts onto wax
    paper and freeze, then lift
    the frozen paste off and
    store in a plastic container.
    Sometimes available in
    tubes, which can be refrig-
    erated and kept after a
    small amount is used.

Vanilla extract

Vinegars
apple cider vinegar (also
    called cider vinegar)
    Made from apple juice; mild
    in flavor.
balsamic or Chinese black
    vinegar
    Balsamic is a mellow,
    slightly sweet Italian aged
    vinegar. (Chinese black vin-
    egar is an acceptable
    substitute.)
red and white wine vinegars
rice wine vinegar
sherry vinegar
    Nutty, and somewhat
    stronger-flavored than most
    wine vinegars. Buy in spe-
    cialty stores.

Wines, liquors (for
    flavoring)
amaretto
anise

kahlua
Madeira
rice wine
sherry
vermouth

IN THE REFRIGERATOR:
Bean curd
    Tofu, or bean curd, is a
    custard-like cake of puréed
    soybeans, bland tasting but
    an excellent protein source.
    It will stay fresh in the re-
    frigerator about a week if
    you change the water daily.
Bread crumbs
    You need never buy these.
    For fresh bread crumbs, use
    fresh or day-old bread; for
    dry, use fresh to 4-day-old
    bread. To dry bread, toast
    in a 250-degree oven until
    golden. Process bread in a
    food processor or blender.
Butter
    Unsalted is best for cooking
    because it does not burn as
    quickly as salted, and it has
    a sweeter flavor. Can be
    kept frozen until needed.
Buttermilk
Cheese
Cheddar cheese, sharp
    A firm cheese, ranging in
    color from nearly white to
    yellow.
cream cheese
Emmenthaler cheese
goat cheese, log type
    Can buy either plain or with
    ash. Goat cheese, or *chèvre*,
    has a distinct, pungent
    taste. The ash gives it a
    slightly salty taste.
Gruyère cheese
Jarlsberg cheese
Monterey Jack cheese
    From California—a mild
    cheese made from skim,
    partly skim, or whole milk.
mozzarella cheese, fresh
    whole milk
    In Italy, the best mozzarella
    comes from the curd of
    water buffalo milk and is
    creamy and sweet tasting.
    In the United States,
    mozzarella is produced from
    whole cow's milk and is a
    stiffer cheese.
Parmesan cheese
    Avoid the preground vari-
    ety: it is very expensive and

almost flavorless. Buy Parmesan by the half- or quarter-pound wedge and grate
as needed: a quarter-pound
produces one cup of grated
cheese. American Par-
mesans are acceptable and
less costly than imported.
Romano is another sub-
stitute—or try mixing the
two.
ricotta cheese
    This white, slightly sweet
    soft cheese is available
    fresh (made from whole
    milk) or dry. It resembles
    good-quality small-curd cot-
    tage cheese, which can be
    substituted.
Romano cheese
Swiss cheese
Corn tortillas
Cream
half-and-half
heavy
sour cream
Eggs
    Will keep up to 6 weeks.
    Before beating eggs, bring
    them to room temperature
    for fluffiest results.
Fruit
apples (red and green)
avocados
lemons
    In addition to its many uses
    in cooking, fresh lemon
    juice, added to cut fruits
    and vegetables, keeps them
    from turning brown.
limes
oranges
Ginger, fresh
    Buy fresh in the produce
    section. Slice only what you
    need. The rest will stay
    fresh in the refrigerator for
    6 weeks wrapped in plastic.
    Or place the whole ginger
    root in a small jar and cover
    it with dry sherry to pre-
    serve it. It will keep almost
    indefinitely.
Mayonnaise
Milk
Mustards
    Select the pungent Dijon
    variety for cooking. The fla-
    vor survives heating.
Puff pastry (frozen)
Vegetables
alfalfa sprouts

artichokes
beets
black-eyed peas
broccoli
carrots
cauliflower
celeriac
celery
cherry tomatoes
Chinese cabbage
    Bok choy, with crisp white
    stalks and dark green
    leaves, and Napa, which has
    wrinkled, pale green leaves,
    are the two kinds of Chinese
    cabbage.
coriander
    Fresh coriander, usually
    sold alongside parsley, has
    similar uses and a hint of
    orange in its taste. It is
    commonly called *cilantro* or
    Chinese parsley. Handle it
    as you would parsley.
corn
cucumber
dill
eggplant
fennel
green beans
green pepper
lettuce
    Boston or Bibb
    butter
    escarole
    radicchio
    Romaine
    sorrel
    spinach
    watercress
lima beans
mirlitons (chayote squash)
mushrooms
parsley
    Put in a glass of water and
    cover loosely with a plastic
    bag. It will keep for a week
    in the refrigerator. Or you
    can wash it, dry it, and re-
    frigerate it in a small plastic
    bag with a dry paper towel
    inside.
peas
potatoes
radishes
red cabbage
red peppers
snow peas
spaghetti squash
tomatillos
tomatoes
zucchini

Yogurt, plain

Equipment

Proper cooking equipment makes the work light and is a good cook's most prized possession. You can cook expertly without a store-bought steamer or even a food processor, but basic pans, knives, and a few other items are indispensable. Below are the things you need and some attractive options for preparing the menus in this volume.

Pots and pans
Large kettle or stockpot
Teakettle
2 large, heavy-gauge skillets (10 to 12 inches in diameter), 1 with cover and ovenproof handle
9- to 10-inch nonstick skillet
2 heavy-gauge sauté pans
3 saucepans with covers (1-, 2-, and 4-quart capacities)
Choose enamel cast iron, plain cast iron, aluminum-clad stainless steel, heavy aluminum (but you need at least two pans that are not aluminum). Best—but very expensive—is tin-lined copper.
2 heavy-gauge, medium-size saucepans with covers
2 woks (or 2 large, heavy-gauge, cast-iron skillets with covers)
Dutch oven
Large broiling tray
Small baking pan
2 rectangular baking dishes, 1 of glass
Porcelain baking dish
Ovenproof casserole with cover
2 baking sheets
Shallow 8-by-12-inch baking sheet
2 cookie sheets
9-inch tart or pie plate
10-inch pie plate
Large steamer unit or improvised steamer
Collapsible vegetable steamer
Chafing dish or fondue pot
Popover mold or muffin tin
Knives
A carbon-steel knife takes a sharp edge but tends to rust. You must wash and dry it after each use; otherwise it can blacken food and counter tops. Good-quality stainless-steel knives, frequently honed, are less trouble and will serve just as well in the home kitchen. Never put a fine knife in the dishwasher. Rinse it, dry it, and put it away—but not loose in a drawer. Knives will stay sharp and last a long time if they have their own storage rack.

Small paring knife (sharp-pointed end)
10- to 12-inch chef's knife
Chinese cleaver

Other cooking tools
Long-handled metal spoon
Long-handled slotted spoon
2 long-handled wooden spoons
Soup ladle
Metal tongs
Wooden tongs
Wooden spatula (for stirring hot ingredients)
Rubber spatula (for folding in hot or cold ingredients, off the heat)
Plastic spatula
Metal spatula
Wide metal spatula
Slotted metal spatula
Metal wok spatula
3 mixing bowls in graduated sizes
3 small bowls
Salad bowl
4 soup bowls or casseroles
2 flat plates
Heatproof serving platter
4 individual soufflé dishes
2 sets of measuring cups and spoons in graduated sizes (one for dry ingredients, another for shortening and liquids)
Strainer
Colander, with a round base (stainless steel, aluminum, or enamel)
Wooden chopping board
Vegetable peeler
Vegetable scrub brush
2 whisks
Kitchen scissors
Pastry brush
Tweezers
Rolling pin
2- or 2½-inch biscuit cutter or round glass
16-inch chopsticks
Cooling rack
Deep fat thermometer

Kitchen timer
Aluminum foil
Paper towels
Plastic wrap
Wax paper
Electric appliances
Blender or food processor
A blender will do most of the work required in this volume, but a food processor will do it more quickly and in larger volume. Food processors should be considered a necessity, not a luxury, for anyone who enjoys cooking.
Electric hand mixer

Optional
Nutmeg grater
Cheese grater (if not using food processor)
Garlic press
Citrus juicer (the inexpensive glass kind from the dime store will do)
Salad spinner
Extra colander (if not using steamer unit or collapsible vegetable steamer)
Sifter (if not using food processor)
Large copper mixing bowl
Chinese mesh spoon
Mortar and pestle
Cheesecloth
4 custard cups
Food mill
Grater

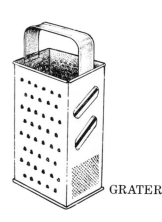

GRATER

STRAINER

SAUCEPANS

CASSEROLE

NUTMEG
GRATER

SAUTÉ PAN

WHISK

PARING KNIFE

CHEF'S KNIFE

VEGETABLE STEAMER

SHARPENING STEEL

VEGETABLE PEELER

LONG-HANDLED WOODEN SPOON

SLOTTED METAL SPOON

METAL COLANDER

Madhur Jaffrey

MENU 1 (Right)
Rice Pilaf with Black-Eyed Peas
and Green Beans
Eggplant in Spicy Tomato Sauce

MENU 2
Persian-Style Rice with Lima Beans and Dill
Cauliflower with Garlic and Sesame Seeds
Yogurt with Tomato and Cucumber

MENU 3
Brown Rice with Mushrooms
Peas and Tomatoes with Cumin Seeds
Yogurt with Mint

C ooking with vegetables and grains is an observance of Hindu religious tradition, which reveres all animal life. Madhur Jaffrey, who is an actress as well as a food writer and cook, learned vegetable cookery in her native India. Vegetables please her spirit and sustain her, she explains. Her three menus guide those who want vegetarian meals that are authentic, simple, and nutritionally balanced. At the heart of Indian cooking is rice—the main dish in each of these menus. As accompaniments, Madhur Jaffrey serves eggplant in a tomato sauce in Menu 1, seasoned cauliflower and a chilled, yogurt-based salad in Menu 2, and a bright mixture of peas and tomatoes along with a minty yogurt in Menu 3.

Like the best Indian cooks, Madhur Jaffrey prepares her vegetables to underscore their natural essence rather than to make them look and taste like meat. She balances her vegetarian meals with nuts, yogurt, and fruits—only a few of the elements in the almost endlessly rich and varied repertoire of Indian cooking—and adds dimension to her recipes by using spices and seasonings, such as whole or ground cumin and coriander seeds, which are an integral part of the cuisine.

The main dish in this festive, all-vegetable Indian meal is rice pilaf with black-eyed peas and green beans, accompanied by a casserole of broiled sliced eggplant in a spicy tomato sauce.

Rice Pilaf with Black-Eyed Peas and Green Beans
Eggplant in Spicy Tomato Sauce

India is famous for rice pilaf, which is rice fried and then braised with vegetables and seasonings. Here Madhur Jaffrey mixes the rice with black-eyed peas and green beans and serves a fennel-flavored eggplant dish on the side.

Frozen black-eyed peas are almost as good as fresh ones and much easier to handle. If you want to use dried peas, you must cook them ahead: Pick through the dried peas to remove unwanted particles, then wash them. Set them to simmer in about 3 inches of water in a large pot. After 2 minutes of simmering, turn the heat off, cover the pot, and let the peas sit for an hour. Then cook them 10 to 20 minutes.

Turmeric, a bright yellow spice in the ginger family, is common on American supermarket shelves, but you may need to shop for whole cumin, coriander, and fennel seeds in a specialty shop or Indian grocery. Fennel seeds have a pleasant, mild licorice taste, like anise, which you can substitute if you reduce the quantity. Frying spices, as in this recipe, helps release and intensify their flavor.

Eggplant soaks up oil when you fry it so broiling the slices with a light brushing of oil cuts down on fat. Broiling also helps eliminate the sometimes bitter taste of eggplant skin. The cook recommends white eggplant for this recipe, or the small Oriental eggplants, but you can use any of the several varieties you may find at the greengrocer.

The tomato sauce for the eggplant slices calls for coarsely chopped fresh ginger. The cook's technique for coarse-chopping ginger is to peel a section of fresh ginger and then slice it thinly. Use a potato masher to smash the ginger slices, then drag them across the surface of the cutting board to break up the fibers.

To make this meal nutritionally complete, include a dessert of fresh fruit with a dairy product. This could be either a platter of fruit, accompanied by a selection of various cheeses, or a bowl of peeled and sliced fresh fruit folded into sweetened yogurt or ice cream.

WHAT TO DRINK

The cook suggests a dry red wine with character, such as an Italian Montepulciano d'Abruzzo, to accompany this lively meal. Cold beer or light ale also would be good.

SHOPPING LIST AND STAPLES

1 large eggplant (about 1½ pounds)
3 medium-size tomatoes
¼ pound green beans
1 medium-size onion
1 lemon
7 medium-size cloves garlic
Fresh ginger
10-ounce package frozen black-eyed peas
¾ cup plus 1 tablespoon vegetable oil
2 cups long-grain rice, preferably basmati
1 tablespoon plus 2 teaspoons ground coriander
1 teaspoon whole cumin seeds
1 teaspoon ground cumin
1 teaspoon whole fennel seeds
¾ teaspoon ground turmeric
½ teaspoon Cayenne pepper
Dash of cinnamon
Salt
Freshly ground pepper

UTENSILS

Food processor or blender
Large skillet with lid
Large, heavy-gauge saucepan or skillet with tight-fitting lid
Medium-size saucepan with lid
Large broiling tray
Large bowl
Small cup
Colander
Measuring cups and spoons
Chef's knife
Paring knife
Wooden spatula
Metal spatula
Pastry brush

START-TO-FINISH STEPS

1. Follow rice pilaf recipe steps 1 through 3. Squeeze enough lemon to measure 2 tablespoons juice, peel and mince garlic, peel and finely chop onion, trim green beans and cut crosswise into ½-inch pieces.

2. Follow rice pilaf recipe steps 4 and 5.

3. Drain rice and follow rice pilaf recipe steps 6 and 7.

4. For eggplant recipe, peel and coarsely chop ginger, peel garlic cloves, and chop tomatoes.

5. Follow eggplant recipe steps 1 through 5.
6. Toss rice and serve with the eggplant.

RECIPES

Rice Pilaf with Black-Eyed Peas and Green Beans

2 cups long-grain rice, preferably basmati
10-ounce package frozen black-eyed peas
2 teaspoons ground coriander
1 teaspoon ground cumin
½ teaspoon ground turmeric
⅛ to ¼ teaspoon Cayenne pepper
¼ teaspoon coarsely ground black pepper
Dash of cinnamon
2 tablespoons lemon juice
4 tablespoons vegetable oil
1 medium-size clove garlic, peeled and minced
1 medium-size onion, peeled and finely chopped
¼ pound green beans, trimmed and cut crosswise into
    ½-inch pieces
1¼ teaspoons salt

1. Place rice in large bowl with cold water to cover. With your hands, swish the rice around quickly; pour off most of the water. Repeat 6 to 8 times, or until water is no longer cloudy. Cover rice with water; set aside 25 minutes.
2. In medium-size saucepan, bring 1½ cups of water to a boil. Add black-eyed peas and return to a boil, breaking up frozen block of peas with fork as they are heating. Cover, turn heat to low, and simmer 10 minutes. Drain peas in colander.
3. While peas are cooking, combine coriander, cumin, turmeric, Cayenne, black pepper, cinnamon, lemon juice, and 1 tablespoon of water in small cup. Mix thoroughly and set aside.
4. In large, heavy-gauge saucepan or skillet, heat oil over medium heat. When hot, add garlic and onion. Cook, stirring with wooden spatula, until onion turns brown at edges.
5. Add spice mixture and stir well to combine. Fry about 1 minute.
6. Add the drained rice, black-eyed peas, green beans, and salt. Cook over medium heat 2 to 3 minutes, stirring carefully so as not to break the grains of rice. Lower heat if rice begins to stick to bottom of pan.

7. Add 3 cups water and bring to a boil. Cover tightly, first with aluminum foil and then with a lid. Turn heat very low and cook 25 minutes. Keep pilaf tightly covered until ready to serve.

Eggplant in Spicy Tomato Sauce

1 large eggplant (about 1½ pounds)
9 tablespoons vegetable oil (approximately)
1 piece fresh ginger (1½ inches by 1 inch), peeled and
    coarsely chopped
6 medium-size cloves garlic, peeled
1 teaspoon whole fennel seeds
1 teaspoon whole cumin seeds
3 medium-size tomatoes, chopped
1 tablespoon ground coriander
1 teaspoon salt
¼ teaspoon ground turmeric
⅛ to ¼ teaspoon Cayenne pepper

1. Preheat broiler.
2. Halve eggplant lengthwise and then cut crosswise into ½-inch slices.
3. Brush slices on both sides with about 3 tablespoons of the oil and arrange them in a single layer in large broiling tray. Broil 3 inches from heat source, about 7 minutes; turn with spatula and broil another 7 minutes, or until eggplant is nicely browned.
4. While eggplant is broiling, purée ginger, garlic, and 3 tablespoons of water in food processor or blender. Set aside. In large skillet, heat remaining 6 tablespoons of oil over medium heat. When hot, add fennel and cumin seeds, and let sizzle 30 seconds, or until seeds turn a shade darker. Add ginger-garlic purée and cook, stirring, 1 minute. Stir in chopped tomatoes, coriander, salt, turmeric, and Cayenne, and bring to a simmer. Cook, still stirring, over medium heat 2 to 3 minutes. Cover, turn heat to low, and cook 5 minutes.
5. Fold the browned eggplant slices into the tomato sauce and bring to a simmer. Cover and cook over low heat another 3 to 5 minutes. Turn into serving dish.

LEFTOVER SUGGESTIONS

If you have leftover eggplant slices, serve them folded into some lightly fork-beaten plain yogurt. To reheat the rice pilaf, sauté it in hot oil with scallions and serve it as a snack or light lunch.

21

Persian-Style Rice with Lima Beans and Dill
Cauliflower with Garlic and Sesame Seeds
Yogurt with Tomato and Cucumber

Colorful plates highlight the muted tones of the Persian rice, sautéed cauliflower, and yogurt-vegetable mixture.

Y ou can buy *basmati* rice in an Indian grocery or specialty food shop; it is aromatic, with delicate, long slender grains. Pick through it carefully before rinsing to remove unwanted particles.

The cauliflower recipe calls for unhulled sesame seeds, which you can buy in a health food store or in an Indian or Chinese market. Be sure to sift through the seeds to

remove any grit before you use them. A precautionary note: when dropped into hot oil, sesame seeds will pop; have a lid or spatter guard handy to hold them in the skillet.

WHAT TO DRINK

A dry white wine is needed for this menu: a French

Mâcon, a California Sauvignon Blanc, or an Italian Chardonnay would all be appropriate choices.

SHOPPING LIST AND STAPLES

1 medium-size cauliflower
1 medium-size ripe tomato
1 medium-size cucumber
1 small onion
5 cloves garlic
Large bunch fresh dill
Small bunch fresh thyme or ½ teaspoon dried
16-ounce container plain yogurt
10-ounce package frozen baby lima beans
½ cup vegetable oil
2 cups long-grain rice, preferably basmati
¼ ounce unhulled sesame seeds
Cayenne pepper
Salt
Freshly ground pepper

UTENSILS

Large skillet
2 large, heavy-gauge saucepans, 1 with tight-fitting lid
Small saucepan
Large bowl
Colander
Measuring cups and spoons
Chef's knife
Paring knife
2 wooden spatulas or spoons
Rubber spatula
Whisk

START-TO-FINISH STEPS

1. Follow Persian-style rice recipe step 1.
2. Follow cauliflower recipe step 1.
3. Follow Persian-style rice recipe step 2.
4. Follow yogurt recipe steps 1 through 3. Refrigerate until ready to serve.
5. Drain rice and follow Persian-style rice recipe steps 3 through 4.
6. Trim cauliflower and break into small flowerets. Follow cauliflower recipe steps 2 through 4.
7. Toss rice and serve with the cauliflower and the yogurt.

RECIPES

Persian-Style Rice with Lima Beans and Dill

2 cups long-grain rice, preferably basmati
10-ounce package frozen baby lima beans
1¼ teaspoons salt
4 tablespoons vegetable oil
1 small onion, peeled and thinly sliced
¾ cup firmly packed chopped fresh dill
1½ teaspoons chopped fresh thyme, or ½ teaspoon dried

1. Place rice in large bowl and wash in several changes of water. Drain in colander. Return rice to bowl and cover with 5 cups of water; set aside 25 minutes.
2. While rice is soaking, cook lima beans in small saucepan in ½ cup water with ¼ teaspoon salt for 8 minutes. Drain in colander.
3. In large, heavy-gauge saucepan, heat oil over medium heat. When hot, add onion. Cook, stirring, until onion is lightly browned. Add drained rice, lima beans, dill, thyme, and remaining salt. Stir gently and cook 2 to 3 minutes, taking care not to break the grains of rice. If rice begins to stick to bottom of pan, turn down heat a bit.
4. Pour in 2⅔ cups of water and bring to a boil. Cover tightly, first with aluminum foil and then with lid. Turn heat to very low and cook 25 minutes. Keep covered until ready to serve.

Cauliflower with Garlic and Sesame Seeds

Salt
1 medium-size cauliflower, broken into small flowerets
4 tablespoons vegetable oil
4 to 5 cloves garlic, peeled and minced
1½ tablespoons unhulled sesame seeds
Dash Cayenne pepper
Freshly ground black pepper

1. In large, heavy-gauge saucepan, bring 3 quarts of water to a boil. Stir in 1 tablespoon salt.
2. Add cauliflower and return water to a rolling boil. Boil rapidly 1 to 1½ minutes, or until cauliflower is crisply tender. Drain in colander and set aside.
3. In large skillet, heat oil over medium heat. When hot, add garlic. Fry, stirring, until garlic turns light brown.
4. Add sesame seeds. When sesame seeds turn a few shades darker or begin to pop, add the cauliflower. Stir cauliflower gently until evenly coated with sesame seeds. Add Cayenne, a generous amount of black pepper, and about ¼ teaspoon salt, and stir once more. Turn into serving bowl.

Yogurt with Tomato and Cucumber

1 medium-size ripe tomato
1 medium-size cucumber
1½ cups plain yogurt
½ teaspoon salt
Freshly ground black pepper
Dash Cayenne pepper

1. Core tomato and cut into ¼-inch dice. Peel cucumber and cut into ½-inch dice.
2. Turn yogurt into serving bowl and beat lightly with fork or whisk until smooth and creamy.
3. Add vegetables and seasonings and mix. Taste and adjust seasonings if necessary.

Brown Rice with Mushrooms
Peas and Tomatoes with Cumin Seeds
Yogurt with Mint

This informal Indian vegetarian meal features brown rice with sliced mushrooms, peas and chopped tomatoes spiced with cumin, and yogurt with chopped mint. Pass the yogurt separately and, if you wish, garnish with sprigs of fresh mint.

Not many Asians eat brown rice. They prefer white because its bland taste does not compete with other savory ingredients. But brown rice, which is unmilled white rice, has a distinctive nutty flavor that appeals to many Westerners. Madhur Jaffrey prefers the texture of long-grain brown rice, but you can use the short-grain variety. To soften it quickly, soak it for 20 minutes in hot water to cover. Remember that brown rice requires a longer cooking time than white, so plan accordingly. The cooked rice dish can stand for a half hour without being ruined. Just remove the foil and replace it with a clean dish towel, which helps to absorb the extra moisture, and set the lid on top of the towel. You can vary this menu and still keep it balanced by substituting whole wheat pita bread for the rice recipe.

The combination of seven spices together with peas and tomatoes is a traditional Delhi dish. In Menus 1 and 2, you fry the spices to bring out their taste, but here you mix them with water into a paste before you fry them.

Mint probably came from Turkey originally, but Indians have adopted it universally. Chopped mint and yogurt, stirred together, cool and refresh the palate after a spicy meal.

If you like, serve fresh fruit, such as melon, berries, mangoes, or pineapple, for dessert.

WHAT TO DRINK

The flavors in this menu would blend best with a small, accommodating red wine, such as an Italian Valpolicella or California Pinot Noir.

SHOPPING LIST AND STAPLES

4 pounds fresh peas
3 ripe tomatoes (about 1¼ pounds total weight)
8 medium-size mushrooms
2 small onions
1 clove garlic
Small bunch parsley
Small bunch mint
16-ounce container plain yogurt
8 tablespoons vegetable oil
1½ cups long-grain brown rice
1 teaspoon brown sugar
2 teaspoons ground coriander
2 teaspoons ground cumin

1 teaspoon whole cumin seeds
½ teaspoon ground turmeric
¼ teaspoon ground ginger
¼ teaspoon freshly grated nutmeg
Cayenne pepper
Salt
Freshly ground black pepper

UTENSILS

Large sauté pan
Large, heavy-gauge saucepan with tight-fitting lid
Large bowl
Small cup
Colander
Measuring cups and spoons
Chef's knife
Paring knife
2 wooden spatulas or spoons
Rubber spatula
Whisk
Nutmeg grater

START-TO-FINISH STEPS

1. Follow brown rice recipe step 1. Peel and mince garlic, peel and chop onion, clean mushrooms with damp paper towels and slice thinly, and mince enough parsley to measure 2 tablespoons.
2. Follow brown rice recipe steps 2 through 5.
3. For peas and tomatoes recipe, grate enough nutmeg to measure ¼ teaspoon, peel and finely chop onion, and core and finely chop tomatoes.
4. Follow peas and tomatoes recipe steps 1 through 7.
5. Prepare yogurt with mint.
6. Toss brown rice and serve with the peas and tomatoes and the yogurt with mint.

RECIPES

Brown Rice with Mushrooms

1½ cups long-grain brown rice
4 tablespoons vegetable oil
1 clove garlic, peeled and minced
1 small onion, peeled and finely chopped
8 medium-size mushrooms, wiped clean and thinly sliced
2 tablespoons minced parsley
1 teaspoon salt

1. Place rice in large bowl and wash in several changes of water. Drain in colander. Return rice to bowl and cover with 3 cups of hot water; set aside 20 minutes.
2. In large, heavy-gauge saucepan, heat oil over medium heat. When hot, add garlic and onion. Fry, stirring, until onion turns brown at edges.
3. Stir in mushrooms and fry them until they wilt.
4. Sprinkle parsley over mixture and stir a few seconds.
5. Add rice with its soaking liquid and salt. Bring to a boil.

Cover tightly, first with aluminum foil and then with lid. Turn heat down to very low and cook 35 minutes. Turn off heat and let pan sit in warm spot, covered and undisturbed, another 5 minutes.

Peas and Tomatoes with Whole Cumin

4 pounds fresh peas (approximately)
2 teaspoons ground cumin
2 teaspoons ground coriander
⅛ to ¼ teaspoon Cayenne pepper
½ teaspoon ground turmeric
¼ teaspoon coarsely ground black pepper
¼ teaspoon ground ginger
¼ teaspoon freshly grated nutmeg
4 tablespoons vegetable oil
1 teaspoon whole cumin seeds
1 small onion, peeled and finely chopped
3 ripe tomatoes, cored and finely chopped (about 1¼ pounds total weight)
1 teaspoon salt
1 teaspoon brown sugar

1. Shell enough peas into a quart measure to make 4 cups. Set aside.
2. In small cup, mix cumin, coriander, Cayenne, turmeric, black pepper, ginger, and nutmeg with 5 tablespoons warm water, and set aside.
3. In large sauté pan, heat oil over medium heat. When hot, add whole cumin seeds. Let them sizzle about 20 seconds.
4. Add chopped onion and fry, stirring, until edges begin to brown.
5. Stir in spice paste and fry with the onion 2 minutes.
6. Add tomatoes. Bring to a vigorous simmer over slightly higher heat. Stir and cook 3 to 4 minutes, or until the tomatoes soften and reduce.
7. Stir in peas, salt, and brown sugar. Bring to a simmer. Cover, turn heat to low, and cook 5 minutes, or until peas are just tender. Turn into serving dish.

Yogurt with Mint

1½ cups plain yogurt
½ to ¾ teaspoon salt
Freshly ground black pepper
Dash Cayenne pepper (optional)
3 tablespoons finely chopped mint

Turn yogurt into serving bowl. Beat lightly with fork or whisk until smooth and creamy. Add remaining ingredients and mix well.

LEFTOVER SUGGESTIONS

Leftover peas and tomatoes become a kind of stew when you add 2 boiled beets, peeled and cut into ½-inch pieces, and some stock or water. Turn the brown rice with mushrooms into a pilaf by heating it in a skillet and adding diced cooked chicken or meat from another meal.

Marlene Sorosky

MENU 1 (Left)
Chicken in Parchment with Mushrooms and Tomatoes
Green Salad with Fried Goat Cheese

MENU 2
Deep-Dish Vegetable Pot Pies
Fresh Orange and Green Salad

MENU 3
Spaghetti Squash with Garden Vegetable Sauce
Almond Popovers with Amaretto Butter

Marlene Sorosky's aim in the kitchen is not merely to cook an enjoyable meal. "I specialize in beautiful food that is varied, uncomplicated, and easy to prepare," says this California-based cooking teacher and author. Vegetables are her particular favorites, since they meet all her requirements for beautiful food. Besides, she believes that vegetables challenge home cooks to be creative; you can season and cook vegetables in an almost infinite number of ways to produce a delicious meal. There are no hard and fast rules with vegetables, she says, advising that you should simply use a common-sense approach.

Each of her three menus demonstrates her "food-should-be-beautiful-yet-simple" philosophy. Baking and serving chicken breasts in parchment packets, as in Menu 1, is an easy but unusual way of handling a familiar dish. The recipe has an added bonus in that it leaves no pots to scrub. The vegetable-and-cheese pot pies of Menu 2 are dramatic with their golden pastry crust, yet they are easy to prepare.

In Menu 3 the spaghetti squash, topped with a red vegetable sauce, is a richly textured main course.

Boneless chicken breasts baked in parchment packets with mushrooms, tomatoes, and cheese make a perfect company meal any time of the year. To get the full impact of the vegetable aroma cut parchment packets open when you serve each person. Fried goat cheese and Romaine lettuce are an appealing side-dish combination.

27

Chicken in Parchment with Mushrooms and Tomatoes
Green Salad with Fried Goat Cheese

For an impressive company dinner that only *looks* complicated, serve chicken breasts with mushrooms, tomatoes, cheese, and a sauce—all assembled and wrapped in parchment packets that puff up as they cook. Kitchen parchment, which is available at specialty food shops and kitchen supply stores, preserves the natural moisture and nutrients of meats and vegetables. It also cuts down on clean-up time, a bonus. As each parchment packet heats up, some steam escapes through the porous paper, so the food does not get soggy. When you are ready to serve the chicken, snip open the packets with scissors to release a burst of aroma.

For the mushroom sauce, you use both chopped fresh mushrooms and the dried Oriental kind to intensify the mushroom flavor of the dish. Dried mushrooms, usually sold in cellophane bags, are available in well-stocked supermarkets or Oriental groceries.

For the salad with fried goat cheese, the cook recommends a log-shaped Montrachet without any black cinder coating. Chilling the crumbly cheese keeps it firm for neat and precise slicing. Freezing the slices, even briefly, helps retain their shape during the frying, which produces a crisp exterior and a soft, creamy interior.

WHAT TO DRINK

The presence of goat cheese in the salad justifies a red wine here: the cook suggests a Cabernet. An Alsatian Gewürztraminer or other crisp white works well also.

SHOPPING LIST AND STAPLES

2 whole boneless, skinless chicken breasts (about 1½ pounds total weight)
½ pound mushrooms
1 head Romaine lettuce
2 small tomatoes
1 onion
3 large cloves garlic
Small bunch fresh parsley
Small bunch fresh basil, or 1 teaspoon dried
1 egg
½ pint heavy cream
2 tablespoons unsalted butter
¼ pound Jarlsberg or Emmenthaler cheese
5 ounces goat cheese, preferably cylindrical
2 tablespoons olive oil
2 tablespoons vegetable oil plus oil for frying
2 tablespoons red wine vinegar
1 teaspoon Dijon mustard
½ ounce dried mushrooms (about 3 mushrooms), preferably Oriental
¼ cup bread crumbs
Salt
Freshly ground pepper
¼ cup Madeira
Parchment paper

UTENSILS

Food processor (optional)
Large skillet
Medium-size skillet
11-by-17-inch cookie sheet
9-inch pie pan
Large flat plate
Small flat plate
Large bowl or glass jar
2 small bowls
Measuring cups and spoons
Chef's knife
Paring knife
Slotted metal spatula
Wooden spoon
Cheese grater (if not using food processor)
Whisk (if not using glass jar)
Scissors
Salad spinner (optional)

START-TO-FINISH STEPS

1. Keep goat cheese refrigerated until ready to use. Slice into eight ¼- to ½-inch rounds. Follow salad recipe step 1.
2. Follow chicken recipe steps 1 and 2. Chop onion, finely chop enough fresh mushrooms to measure 2 cups, crush garlic with flat side of chef's knife, chop parsley and basil, if using fresh basil, and core and thinly slice tomatoes. Using grater or food processor fitted with shredding disk, shred cheese.
3. Follow salad recipe steps 2 and 3.
4. Follow chicken recipe steps 3 through 7.
5. Follow salad recipe steps 4 and 5.
6. Follow chicken recipe step 8 and bring to the table with the salad.

Chicken in Parchment with Mushrooms and Tomatoes

½ ounce dried mushrooms (about 3 mushrooms), preferably Oriental
2 whole skinless, boneless chicken breasts (about 1½
  pounds total weight)
2 tablespoons unsalted butter
1 onion, chopped
½ pound fresh mushrooms, finely chopped (about 2 cups)
3 large cloves garlic, crushed
¼ cup chopped fresh parsley
1 tablespoon chopped fresh basil, or 1 teaspoon dried
Salt
Freshly ground pepper
¼ cup Madeira
¼ cup heavy cream
2 small tomatoes, cored and thinly sliced
½ cup shredded Jarlsberg or Emmenthaler cheese

1. In small bowl, soak dried mushrooms in hot water to cover for 10 minutes. Drain off liquid and reserve for another use. Rinse mushrooms and cut off and discard tough stems. Finely chop the mushrooms.
2. Trim chicken breasts of any fat and split in half.
3. In medium-size skillet, melt butter and sauté onion until soft. Add the dried and fresh mushrooms, garlic, parsley, basil, 1 teaspoon salt, and pepper to taste. Cook, stirring occasionally, until mixture is almost dry, about 7 minutes. Add Madeira and cook until evaporated, about 4 minutes. Remove pan from heat and stir in heavy cream. Season to taste.
4. Preheat oven to 475 degrees.
5. Cut 4 pieces of parchment paper into heart shapes approximately 12 inches long and 12 inches wide at top. (See diagram below.) Unfold each heart and place 1 chicken breast half along centerfold of each parchment heart. Sprinkle with salt and pepper.
6. Spoon an equal portion of mushroom mixture over each chicken breast half, mounding it slightly. Place 3 or 4 overlapping tomato slices over each serving and sprinkle each with 2 tablespoons of cheese.
7. Refold each heart and seal packages by starting at rounded end, rolling and crimping edges together tightly. Twist tip of heart to seal. Place packages on baking sheet, taking care not to overlap them. Bake in center or lower third of oven 10 to 12 minutes; they should be puffed and lightly browned.
8. Remove from oven. Place on individual plates and, with scissors, cut an X in top of each package. Fold back corners and serve.

Green Salad with Fried Goat Cheese

1 egg
1 teaspoon water
¼ cup dry bread crumbs
5 ounces goat cheese, chilled and cut into 8 slices,
  each ¼ to ½ inch thick
1 head Romaine lettuce
2 tablespoons vegetable oil
2 tablespoons olive oil
1 teaspoon Dijon mustard
2 tablespoons red wine vinegar
Salt and freshly ground pepper
Vegetable oil for frying

1. In small bowl, beat together egg and water. Place bread crumbs on small, flat plate. Dip cheese slices in the beaten egg and coat with the bread crumbs. Place the coated slices in pie pan. Cover with foil and leave in freezer at least 30 minutes.
2. Wash lettuce and dry in salad spinner or pat dry with paper towels. Tear into bite-size pieces, wrap in kitchen towel, and refrigerate until ready to serve.
3. For salad dressing, combine vegetable oil, olive oil, mustard, vinegar, and salt and pepper to taste in large bowl or glass jar; whisk or shake until blended. Set aside.
4. In large skillet, add vegetable oil to depth of ¼ inch and heat over moderate heat. Test oil by dropping in a cube of bread: if it browns lightly in 40 seconds, the oil is hot enough. Remove cheese slices from freezer and fry about 3 minutes per side, or until crisp and evenly browned. Remove to paper-towel-lined plate.
5. Remove lettuce from refrigerator, shake or whisk dressing to recombine, and toss salad with the dressing. Divide among 4 dinner or salad plates and top each serving with 2 slices of the fried goat cheese.

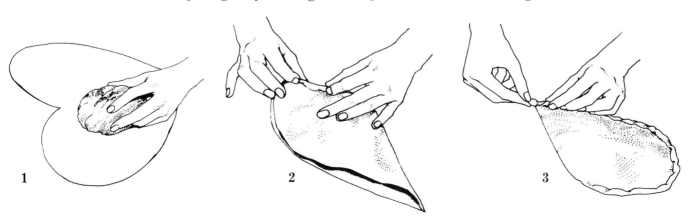

1   2   3

Deep-Dish Vegetable Pot Pies
Fresh Orange and Green Salad

For an informal meal, offer vegetable pot pies with puff pastry crusts and a salad of orange sections and chopped avocado.

W hen Marlene Sorosky devised this home-style, economical meal, she wanted to serve a medley of familiar vegetables in an unusual way, so she baked them in individual pot pies with puff-pastry crusts. These pies look elegant enough for company yet are wonderful for a family meal, too. All the vegetables are easy to cut up for sautéing except the onions, which you must peel. To peel them easily, the cook suggests that you first cut a small "x" at the root end with a sharp paring knife, then place them in a pot of boiling water. Let the water return to a boil and cook the onions 3 to 5 minutes. Their skins will slip right off.

Marlene Sorosky says there are no binding rules for the vegetables you use. Be flexible and let the season guide you: choose asparagus and fresh peas in spring, zucchini and tomatoes in summer. Just use the same proportions. Although you can assemble and bake these pot pies in an hour, you can do them ahead and freeze them, unbaked, for another evening. For handling frozen puff pastry, follow package directions.

The salad of orange segments, cubed avocado, and leaf lettuce is a colorful accompaniment to the vegetable pot pie entrée. Its tart, sweet dressing provides a flavor contrast to the mildly seasoned main course. By adding crunchy poppy seeds to the dressing, Marlene Sorosky also adds flavor and texture to the salad.

WHAT TO DRINK

Light young wines, either red or white, are best with this menu. The cook recommends either a California Pinot Noir or Sauvignon Blanc, but dry Chenin Blanc or Pinot Blanc are also fine choices.

SHOPPING LIST AND STAPLES

1 bunch broccoli
9 small white onions
½ pound mushrooms
1 head Boston or butter lettuce
1 ripe avocado
3 small navel oranges
Small bunch fresh basil, or 1 teaspoon dried
Combination of fresh parsley, chives, tarragon, and
    chervil, or 1 teaspoon dried *fines herbes*
1 egg
½ pint half-and-half
1 stick unsalted butter
6 ounces Swiss cheese
¼ pound Parmesan cheese
¼ cup oil, preferably peanut oil
2 tablespoons apple cider vinegar
¼ cup all-purpose flour
1 pound frozen puff pastry
9-ounce package frozen artichoke hearts
Hot pepper sauce
¼ ounce poppy seeds
¼ teaspoon dry mustard
Salt and freshly ground pepper
⅓ cup dry white wine or dry vermouth

UTENSILS

Food processor or blender
Medium-size skillet
Large saucepan
8-by-12-inch shallow baking sheet
4 heatproof soup bowls or casseroles
Small bowl
Measuring cups and spoons
Chef's knife
Paring knife
Wooden spoon
Rolling pin
Cheese grater (if not using food processor)
Whisk
Pastry brush
Salad spinner (optional)

START-TO-FINISH STEPS

1. Thaw artichoke hearts and ½ pound puff pastry.
2. Rinse broccoli, trim stems, and break or cut into small flowerets. With paring knife, peel and slice onions. Clean mushrooms with damp paper towels and slice. If using fresh herbs, chop enough basil to measure 1 tablespoon and chop the other fresh herbs to measure 1 tablespoon. Using grater or food processor fitted with shredding disk, shred Swiss cheese and then, using metal blade, grate Parmesan.
3. Follow vegetable pies recipe steps 1 through 8.
4. About 15 minutes before vegetable pies are done, prepare salad. Peel 2 oranges, paring away the white pith, and break oranges into segments. Squeeze another orange to measure 2 tablespoons juice. Peel and mince enough onion to measure 1 tablespoon. Peel and cube avocado.
5. Follow salad steps 1 and 2, and bring to the table with the vegetable pot pies.

RECIPES

Deep-Dish Vegetable Pot Pies

1 stick unsalted butter
1 bunch broccoli, cut into bite-size flowerets
8 small white onions, peeled and sliced
½ pound mushrooms, sliced
¼ cup all-purpose flour
⅓ cup dry white wine or dry vermouth
1 cup half-and-half
Several dashes hot pepper sauce
½ teaspoon salt
Freshly ground pepper
1 tablespoon chopped fresh basil, or 1 teaspoon dried
1 tablespoon combined chopped fresh parsley, chives,
    tarragon, and chervil,
    or 1 teaspoon dried *fines herbes*
1½ cups shredded Swiss cheese

½ cup freshly grated Parmesan cheese
9-ounce package frozen artichoke hearts, defrosted
½ pound frozen puff pastry, defrosted until pliable, but
   still refrigerated
1 egg

1. In medium-size skillet, melt 4 tablespoons of the butter. Add broccoli, onions, and mushrooms, and cook, tossing and stirring with wooden spoon, 5 minutes.
2. In large saucepan, melt remaining butter. Stir in flour and whisk over low heat 1 to 2 minutes, or until bubbling. Remove from heat and whisk in wine and half-and-half.
3. Return pan to heat and bring to a boil, whisking constantly. Stir in hot pepper sauce, salt, pepper to taste, and herbs.
4. Remove pan from heat and cool slightly. Stir in the cheeses, vegetable mixture, and artichoke hearts. Divide mixture among 4 heatproof soup bowls or casseroles.
5. Preheat oven to 400 degrees.
6. On lightly floured board, roll 1 sheet puff pastry about ¼ inch thick. Measure diameter of bowls; with sharp knife, cut out 4 pastry circles, each 1 to 2 inches larger than the tops of the bowls.
7. In small bowl, lightly beat egg with 1 tablespoon water. With your fingers, brush rims of bowls with the egg wash. Place a pastry circle over top of each bowl, pressing pastry over edge so that it extends at least ¾ inch over sides. Press down with fork tines to seal. Brush pastry with egg wash. If desired, make decorations such as flowers or leaves with any extra pastry dough; press on top of pastry circles and brush with egg wash. You may need a second sheet of pastry dough for 4 bowls.
8. Place bowls on shallow baking sheet. Bake 20 to 25 minutes, or until pastry is puffed and browned. Let rest 10 minutes before serving.

Fresh Orange and Green Salad

1 head Boston or butter lettuce
2 small navel oranges, peeled and broken into segments
1 ripe avocado, peeled and cut into cubes
1 tablespoon minced onion
2 tablespoons apple cider vinegar
2 tablespoons orange juice
¼ cup oil, preferably peanut oil
1 teaspoon poppy seeds
¼ teaspoon dry mustard
1 teaspoon salt

1. Wash lettuce and dry in salad spinner or pat dry with paper towels. Tear into bite-size pieces and place in salad bowl. Add orange segments and avocado.
2. Combine onion, vinegar, orange juice, oil, poppy seeds, mustard, and salt in food processor or blender and process until well blended. Toss salad with just enough dressing to coat lettuce and orange segments. Refrigerate any remaining dressing to use another time.

ADDED TOUCH

This dessert can be assembled ahead and baked while you are eating the vegetable pot pies and salad. Be sure to turn the oven temperature down to 350 degrees after removing the vegetable pies.

Baked Pears

4 soft ripe pears, preferably Anjou
2 tablespoons sour cream, plus additional sour cream for
   garnish (optional)
½ cup brown sugar, firmly packed
4 tablespoons unsalted butter, at room temperature
6 tablespoons dark rum

1. Preheat oven to 350 degrees.
2. Peel, quarter, and core pears. Lay each quarter on its side in shallow casserole so that pears fit snugly in single layer.
3. Dot pears with 2 tablespoons sour cream and sprinkle with brown sugar. Dot with bits of butter and pour rum over pears. Cover with foil and bake 25 to 35 minutes, or until pears are barely tender when pierced with a fork. Serve warm, spooning the pan juices over the pears. Top each serving with additional dollop of sour cream, if desired.

LEFTOVER SUGGESTION

You will have ½ pound of frozen puff pastry left over from the vegetable pies. Save it for the next time you prepare pot pies, or use the pastry for a fruit tart. Thaw pastry, then roll out into two 8-inch rounds, each ¼ inch thick. Cut out the center from one of the rounds, leaving a 1-inch border. Place that border on top of the other uncut round, and place them on a buttered cookie sheet. Bake in a preheated 400-degree oven 20 to 25 minutes, or until the shell puffs and browns. Let cool, then fill the center with cut-up fresh fruit and top with whipped cream.

Spaghetti Squash with Garden Vegetable Sauce
Almond Popovers with Amaretto Butter

The vegetable sauce is a colorful contrast to the pale strands of spaghetti squash. Serve popovers with almond-flavored butter.

The cooked flesh of spaghetti squash forms long strands that look like golden-orange pasta. To cook the squash, you can boil it whole or, if you prefer, slice it in half lengthwise, set the halves cut side down in a shallow baking dish filled with 1½ inches of water, and bake the halves at 375 degrees 30 to 40 minutes, or until the flesh becomes tender. When the cooked squash is cool enough to handle, rake through the flesh with fork tines to produce the pasta-like strands. You can refrigerate the strands for later use or serve them immediately. These crunchy strands are very mildly flavored, which makes them a perfect base for the rich vegetable-and-chicken sauce.

If you buy a squash that weighs more than two pounds, it may be difficult to cut in half unless you use a heavy cleaver. The cook suggests that you ask your produce man to halve it for you. You can refrigerate the uncooked half for later use or bake the whole squash at once and save the cooked strands for another day.

To save time, you can make the popover batter a day ahead; just stir it well before you pour it into the muffin tin or custard cups. The delicately sweet almond butter for the popovers calls for Amaretto, an almond-flavored Italian liqueur. If you wish, you can eliminate both the Amaretto and the confectioners' sugar from the butter recipe and substitute ¼ cup honey. Crunchy almonds sprinkled on top add texture and flavor.

WHAT TO DRINK

The cook favors a Sauvignon Blanc with this menu, but its piquant flavors would go equally well with a simple Chianti or a California Gamay.

SHOPPING LIST AND STAPLES

3 boneless, skinless chicken breast halves (about 1¼ pounds total weight)
1 medium-size spaghetti squash (about 2 pounds)
1 small eggplant
½ pound mushrooms
1 small green pepper
1 large stalk celery
1 medium-size onion
2 cloves garlic
2 large eggs
1 cup milk
1 stick unsalted butter
¼ pound Parmesan cheese
16-ounce can whole tomatoes in thick tomato purée
6-ounce can tomato paste
¼ cup olive oil
¼ teaspoon almond extract
1 cup all-purpose flour
2 tablespoons confectioners' sugar
2½-ounce package whole blanched almonds
1 bay leaf
½ teaspoon dried basil
½ teaspoon dried thyme
½ teaspoon dried oregano
Salt and freshly ground pepper
2 teaspoons Amaretto liqueur

UTENSILS

Food processor or blender
Stockpot
Large, non-aluminum saucepan
15½-by-12-inch cookie sheet
6 custard cups, popover mold, or heavy-gauge muffin tin
Medium-size bowl
Small bowl
Measuring cups and spoons
Chef's knife
Paring knife
2 wooden spoons
Rubber spatula
Electric hand mixer (optional)
Cheese grater (if not using food processor)
Metal tongs

START-TO-FINISH STEPS

1. Follow spaghetti squash recipe step 1.
2. Follow almond popovers recipe steps 1 through 3. Bring butter for Amaretto butter recipe to room temperature.
3. Follow spaghetti squash recipe step 2.
4. Dice chicken, peel and cut up eggplant, and clean mushrooms with damp paper towels and slice. Chop onion, celery, green pepper, and tomatoes. Crush garlic cloves with flat side of chef's knife. Using food processor or cheese grater, grate Parmesan cheese and set aside.
5. Bake popovers, step 4.
6. Follow spaghetti squash recipe steps 3 through 5.
7. Prepare Amaretto butter, steps 1 and 2.
8. Follow spaghetti squash recipe step 6, popovers recipe step 5, and bring to the table at once with the Amaretto butter.

RECIPES

Spaghetti Squash with Garden Vegetable Sauce

1 medium-size spaghetti squash (about 2 pounds)
¼ cup olive oil
3 boneless, skinless chicken breast halves, cut in ½-inch dice
1 medium-size onion, chopped
1 small eggplant, peeled and cut into ¾-inch pieces
2 cups thickly sliced mushrooms
1 large stalk celery, coarsely chopped (about 1 cup)
½ cup coarsely chopped green pepper
16-ounce can whole tomatoes in thick tomato purée, chopped
3 ounces (½ can) tomato paste
2 cloves garlic, crushed
½ teaspoon dried basil
½ teaspoon dried thyme

½ teaspoon dried oregano
1 bay leaf
1 teaspoon salt
Freshly ground pepper
Freshly grated Parmesan cheese

1. Bring large stockpot of water to a boil.
2. Place spaghetti squash in pot and cook 20 to 30 minutes, or until tender when pierced with a fork.
3. Meanwhile, heat olive oil in large, non-aluminum saucepan over medium heat. Add chicken, onion, and eggplant, and cook, stirring occasionally, until the onion is soft, about 10 minutes.
4. Stir in mushrooms, celery, and green pepper, and cook, stirring, until celery is barely tender, about 4 minutes.
5. Add chopped tomatoes and purée, tomato paste, garlic, and seasonings. Simmer uncovered, stirring occasionally, 20 minutes, or until sauce thickens slightly. Remove bay leaf.
6. When squash is tender, remove from pot with tongs. Cut in half lengthwise. Discard seeds and pull out squash strands with a fork. Mound squash strands on serving platter and spoon sauce over them. Sprinkle lightly with Parmesan cheese and pass additional cheese at the table, if desired.

Almond Popovers with Amaretto Butter

¼ cup whole blanched almonds
1 cup all-purpose flour
1 cup milk
2 large eggs
Dash salt
Amaretto butter (see following recipe)

1. Preheat oven to 325 degrees. Toast almonds on cookie sheet until lightly browned, about 3 to 5 minutes. Cool; sliver enough to measure 2 tablespoons and reserve 1 tablespoon for Amaretto butter garnish. Turn oven to 425 degrees.
2. In medium-size bowl, mix together flour, 1 tablespoon almonds, milk, eggs, and salt with wooden spoon until well blended. The batter may be slightly lumpy.
3. Thoroughly butter 6 custard cups, popover mold, or heavy-gauge muffin tin. Fill two thirds full with batter.
4. Bake popovers 30 to 35 minutes, or until puffed and browned.
5. Remove from oven and arrange popovers in a bread basket. Serve immediately with Amaretto butter.

Amaretto Butter

1 stick unsalted butter, at room temperature
2 tablespoons confectioners' sugar
2 teaspoons Amaretto liqueur
¼ teaspoon almond extract
1 tablespoon toasted, blanched, slivered almonds for garnish

1. In food processor or blender, process butter and sugar or, using hand mixer, beat butter and sugar in small bowl until thoroughly blended. Slowly add Amaretto and almond extract, mixing until incorporated.
2. Turn into small serving bowl; sprinkle with slivered almonds.

ADDED TOUCH

Although you can prepare this dessert quickly, you must make it far enough in advance to allow it to freeze.

Fresh Pineapple Ice

½ fresh pineapple
2 tablespoons sugar
1 tablespoon lemon juice
2 tablespoons kirsch

1. Halve, core, and peel pineapple half. Cut into 1-inch chunks and purée in 2 batches in food processor or blender. There should be about 2 cups of purée. (If you have less than 2 cups, reduce sugar to taste.)
2. Stir in ½ cup of water, sugar, lemon juice, and kirsch. Spoon the purée into divided ice cube trays. Freeze until solid, at least 2 hours.
3. Before serving, process 4 to 6 of the pineapple cubes at a time in food processor or blender. Turn machine on and off until cubes are broken up. Process until mixture becomes a velvety slush.
4. Spoon into bowls and serve immediately.

LEFTOVER SUGGESTION

Leftover cooked strands of spaghetti squash are good cold in a salad dressed with a tangy vinaigrette. If you prefer, reheat the strands in a vegetable steamer, then toss them with butter and Parmesan cheese. Or, stir fry the strands, adding cooked vegetables and diced chicken. Heat the mixture thoroughly.

Beverly Cox

MENU 1 (Right)
Eggplant Pie
Green Bean and Onion Salad
Oranges with Cinnamon

MENU 2
**Louisiana-Style Mirlitons Stuffed with Ham
and Shrimp**
Marinated Carrots

MENU 3
**Chicken Breasts with a Bouquet of Vegetables
and Sweet-and-Sour Sauce**
Green Salad with Herbed Vinaigrette

To Beverly Cox, a perfectly cooked meal must be nutritionally balanced as well as delicious and artistic. She adapts her classic French training to a lighter style of cooking that focuses on garden-fresh produce. She experiments with converting vegetable side dishes into complete main courses, often turning to the Cajun cooking of Louisiana for ideas.

Because she likes vegetables slightly undercooked, Beverly Cox relies on two methods for cooking them: steaming and quick-boiling. Steaming preserves the nutrients, colors, and crunchy textures of vegetables, as well as prevents them from becoming waterlogged. On the other hand, quick-boiling has its advantages, too. It tenderizes vegetables and diminishes the tart or bitter taste of some. After you remove the vegetables from the boiling water, "refresh" them—that is, dunk them into cold water, which stops the cooking and sets the color.

The entrées in the first two menus are substantial vegetable dishes. The eggplant pie of Menu 1 is a good example of a vegetable main course that can stand on its own nutritionally. In Menu 2, mirlitons, green pear-shaped squash, are stuffed with shrimp, ham, and seasonings for a satisfying Louisiana-style dish. Beverly Cox seasons the stuffing with Cajun red-pepper sauce.

Even though the entrée in Menu 3 cooks at once in one pot, it is not a stew. This energy-efficient cooking method is a legacy from Oriental kitchens, where cooks often steam and lightly poach their foods. A particular bonus is that there is only one pot to clean.

This substantial menu, ideal for a company lunch, is rich with color and texture. Sprinkle the baked eggplant pie with grated Parmesan cheese just before you serve it, if you wish. Pass the bundles of green beans, held by red pepper rings, on a serving dish or on chilled salad plates. Orange sections with cinnamon come to the table in a serving bowl.

Eggplant Pie
Green Bean and Onion Salad
Oranges with Cinnamon

This main-course eggplant pie resembles a quiche, but it is baked without a pastry crust; instead, Beverly Cox forms the crust from unpeeled eggplant slices to hold the cheese-egg-vegetable filling. When shopping, select eggplants that feel heavy and have smooth, flawless, shiny purple skins. Brown rough spots indicate probable decay or improper handling. Refrigerated, eggplant can keep up to six weeks. Because eggplant that is not perfectly ripe can taste bitter, Beverly Cox calls for parboiling the slices for several minutes to render any bitter juices. You can peel or not peel the eggplant as you wish: remember that the skin adds some flavor and also helps keep the slices intact.

The dessert—orange slices sparked with ground cinnamon—is a Moroccan combination. To make this fruit salad, select seedless oranges. When you peel them, remove as much bitter white pith as possible. Use a sharp paring knife to peel the skin off in a spiral, following the contours of the fruit.

WHAT TO DRINK

The brightness of the flavors in this menu call for a fresh and fruity red wine, such as an Italian Dolcetto or a California Gamay.

SHOPPING LIST AND STAPLES

5 large, ripe tomatoes or 16-ounce can whole tomatoes
1 pound green beans
1 medium-size eggplant (approximately ½ pound)
1 large red bell pepper
4 lettuce leaves (optional)
4 oranges
1 large lemon
1 onion
Small bunch scallions
1 clove garlic
Fresh parsley sprigs
4 eggs
8 ounces mozzarella
¼ pound Romano cheese
½ cup plus 3 tablespoons olive oil
2 teaspoons red wine vinegar
2 teaspoons Dijon mustard
3½-ounce jar capers

Honey (optional)
Sugar (optional)
¼ teaspoon dried oregano
¼ teaspoon dried basil
Cinnamon
Salt and freshly ground pepper

UTENSILS

Large skillet
Large saucepan with cover
Small saucepan (if using fresh tomatoes)
10-inch pie plate
2 medium-size mixing bowls
Small mixing bowl
Colander
Vegetable steamer
Measuring cups and spoons
Chef's knife
Paring knife
Wooden spoon
Rubber spatula
2 whisks
Electric hand mixer
Cheese grater

START-TO-FINISH STEPS

1. Follow eggplant pie recipe step 1. While water comes to a boil, peel and halve garlic, mince enough onion to measure 3 tablespoons, and mince enough parsley to measure 1 tablespoon. If using canned tomatoes, peel, if necessary, and seed and chop them. If using fresh tomatoes, blanch them 30 seconds in small saucepan of boiling water. Then peel, seed, and chop.
2. Follow eggplant pie recipe steps 2 through 7.
3. While sauce is cooking, follow salad recipe steps 1 through 5, using large saucepan just used for parboiling eggplant.
4. Slice mozzarella and tomato, and follow eggplant pie recipe steps 8 through 13.
5. Follow salad recipe steps 6 through 8.
6. Prepare oranges recipe, steps 1 through 5.
7. Grate cheese and follow eggplant pie recipe step 14.
8. Follow salad recipe step 9.
9. Follow eggplant pie recipe step 15 and serve with green bean salad. Serve oranges with cinnamon for dessert.

Eggplant Pie

1 medium-size eggplant (approximately ½ pound)
1 clove garlic, peeled and halved
3 tablespoons olive oil
Salt
Freshly ground pepper
3 tablespoons minced onion
2 cups peeled, seeded, and chopped tomatoes, canned or
    fresh (about 4 whole tomatoes)
1 tablespoon minced fresh parsley
¼ teaspoon dried oregano
¼ teaspoon dried basil
8 ounces thinly sliced mozzarella
6 tomato slices (about 1 large tomato)
2 whole eggs
1 teaspoon capers
2 egg whites
1 tablespoon freshly grated Romano cheese

1. In large covered saucepan, bring 1 quart of water to a boil.
2. Preheat oven to 375 degrees.
3. Rinse eggplant and slice into ½-inch rounds. Parboil slices 3 minutes, drain in colander, and pat dry, squeezing out excess moisture with paper towels.
4. Rub inside of 10-inch pie plate with halved clove of garlic; discard garlic. Pour in 2 tablespoons of the olive oil. Coat both sides of the eggplant slices with the oil and arrange them in pie plate so that they cover bottom and extend partway up sides. Sprinkle lightly with salt and pepper.
5. Place pie plate on middle rack in oven while you prepare the tomato mixture.
6. In large skillet, heat remaining 1 tablespoon olive oil. Add onion and sauté until onion is transparent and soft.
7. Add chopped tomatoes, parsley, oregano, basil, and salt and pepper to taste. Cook over medium heat, stirring often, until sauce cooks down and thickens slightly, about 10 minutes.
8. After sauce has thickened, remove eggplant from oven. Cover eggplant with mozzarella slices and top with tomato slices.
9. Crack whole eggs into medium-size mixing bowl. Whisk until light and frothy.
10. Stir tomato mixture into the eggs. Add capers and salt and pepper to taste.
11. Using electric hand mixer, beat egg whites with pinch of salt in separate bowl until they form soft peaks.
12. Gently fold the egg whites into the tomato-egg mixture until thoroughly incorporated.
13. Pour mixture into pie plate and bake on rack in middle of oven 20 minutes.
14. Sprinkle with grated cheese and return to oven for 5 to 10 minutes more, or until eggs are thoroughly set and top is lightly browned.
15. Remove pie from oven; cool a few minutes. Cut pie into wedges and serve.

Green Bean and Onion Salad

1 pound green beans
1 large red bell pepper
3 small or 2 large scallions
1 large lemon
2 teaspoons red wine vinegar
2 teaspoons Dijon mustard
½ cup olive oil
Salt and freshly ground pepper
4 lettuce leaves for garnish (optional)

1. In saucepan fitted with collapsible vegetable steamer, bring 1 inch of water to a boil.
2. Rinse beans, pepper, and scallions under cold running water.
3. Remove strings from beans and trim ends. Steam beans, covered, until just tender, about 3 to 4 minutes.
4. While beans are cooking, wash pepper; core and seed through stem end, leaving shell intact. Cut pepper shell into thin rings; set aside.
5. Place beans in colander and refresh them under cold running water.
6. Slice scallions into thin rings. You should have about 3 tablespoons. Squeeze lemon to measure 3½ teaspoons juice. Reserve 1½ teaspoons for oranges recipe.
7. In small mixing bowl, combine 2 teaspoons lemon juice, wine vinegar, and mustard. Add olive oil in a slow, steady stream, whisking constantly.
8. Place the well-drained beans in flat serving bowl and toss with the dressing and scallions. Sprinkle with salt and pepper to taste. Marinate 15 minutes before serving.
9. When ready to assemble, group the beans in small bundles. Slip a red pepper ring around the center of each bundle. To serve, place the bundles on chilled serving platter, lined with lettuce leaves, if desired. Sprinkle scallions and any dressing remaining in bowl over the bundles.

Oranges with Cinnamon

4 oranges
1½ teaspoons lemon juice
Cinnamon
Honey or sugar (optional)
Crisp nut cookies for accompaniment (optional)

1. Peel oranges, removing all the white inner skin.
2. Holding a peeled orange over a serving bowl to catch the juice, cut with sharp paring knife between section membranes and let sections fall into bowl.
3. Squeeze remaining membranes to remove any juice. Discard membranes. Repeat with remaining oranges.
4. Add reserved lemon juice to the orange sections and sprinkle with cinnamon to taste.
5. Check for sweetness and add honey or sugar to taste, if desired. Cover and refrigerate until ready to serve for dessert. If you wish, serve with crisp nut cookies.

Louisiana-Style Mirlitons Stuffed with Ham and Shrimp
Marinated Carrots

Arrange this Southern-style meal of ham-and-shrimp-stuffed mirlitons and marinated carrot slices on individual dinner plates. Garnish the carrots with chopped parsley or sliced scallions, or both.

S outhern cooks often use a pear-shaped winter squash called mirliton, also known as chayote squash in the West Indies, Mexico, and the Southwest. This green squash tastes somewhat like a cucumber and is a good flavor contrast for savory fillings. Many supermarkets and greengrocers nationwide now stock mirlitons. If you cannot find them, you can use green bell peppers. If so, parboil the peppers before you stuff and bake them. Or, you can substitute any winter squash (except spaghetti squash). The tastes will differ, but the textures will be similar. When you shop for this meal, select mirlitons that are dark green and firm. You can store them for up to two weeks in the refrigerator.

The ham-and-shrimp stuffing, seasoned with onion, garlic, herbs, and hot-pepper sauce, is Louisiana style: ham and shrimp are ubiquitous ingredients there, as is the piquant pepper sauce.

The carrots, which Beverly Cox often has enjoyed in the South, make an unusual salad or side dish. It is important that you select firm carrots of uniform size for the fullest flavor and the most attractive slices. After peeling the carrots, cut them on the bias into inch-thick pieces and steam them until just tender. The steaming makes them porous enough to absorb some of the vinaigrette. Serve the salad at room temperature for maximum flavor.

WHAT TO DRINK

The harmony of ingredients here demands a medium-bodied, not-too-obtrusive white wine, such as an Entre-Deux-Mers or a young white Bordeaux.

SHOPPING LIST AND STAPLES

½ pound cooked ham
¾ pound fresh shrimp
4 small or 2 large mirlitons (chayote squash)
1 pound carrots
1 large onion
Small bunch scallions
Small bunch fresh parsley
Small bunch fresh thyme, or pinch dried thyme
1 large clove garlic
3 tablespoons unsalted butter
5 tablespoons olive oil
2 tablespoons red wine vinegar
¼ teaspoon hot pepper sauce

¼ loaf day-old French or other white bread
¼ teaspoon dried oregano
Salt
Freshly ground black pepper

UTENSILS

Food processor or blender
Large skillet
Large saucepan with lid
Baking sheet
Medium-size bowl
Colander
Vegetable steamer
Measuring cups and spoons
Chef's knife
Paring knife
Wooden spoon
Wide metal spatula
Tongs
Vegetable peeler
Small kitchen scissors (optional)

START-TO-FINISH STEPS

1. Follow mirlitons recipe steps 1 and 2.
2. For mirlitons recipe, rinse shrimp in colander. Using sharp paring knife or small pair of scissors, peel and devein shrimp. Dice shrimp and ham, peel and finely chop enough onion to measure ⅔ cup, peel and mince garlic clove, mince enough parsley to measure 1 tablespoon, and, if using fresh thyme, mince a few sprigs to measure ¼ teaspoon. Process enough bread in food processor or blender to measure 1 cup bread crumbs. Lightly grease baking sheet.
3. Follow mirlitons recipe steps 3 through 8.
4. While the mirlitons are baking, follow marinated carrots recipe steps 1 through 5, using steamer used for mirlitons.
5. Follow mirlitons recipe step 9 and marinated carrots recipe step 6, and bring to the table.

RECIPES

Louisiana-Style Mirlitons Stuffed with Ham and Shrimp

4 small or 2 large mirlitons (chayote squash)
3 tablespoons unsalted butter
¾ pound fresh shrimp, peeled, deveined, and finely diced
½ pound cooked ham, finely diced
⅔ cup finely chopped onion
1 large clove garlic, minced
¼ teaspoon hot pepper sauce
1 tablespoon minced fresh parsley
¼ teaspoon minced fresh thyme, or pinch dried thyme
Salt
Freshly ground black pepper

1 cup unseasoned fresh bread crumbs, preferably freshly made from day-old French or white bread (about ¼ loaf)
Vegetable oil or butter for greasing baking sheet

1. In large covered saucepan fitted with collapsible vegetable steamer, bring 1 inch of water to a boil.
2. Cut squash in half and remove seeds. Steam halves, cut side down, 30 to 35 minutes, or until they are tender but still hold their shape. Check water level occasionally, adding more water if necessary.
3. While mirlitons are steaming, melt 2 tablespoons of the butter in large skillet. Add shrimp, ham, onion, garlic, and hot pepper sauce, and cook over medium heat, stirring often with a wooden spoon, until onions become transparent.
4. Preheat oven to 375 degrees.
5. Using tongs, remove squash and drain on paper towels. Carefully scoop out pulp into medium-size bowl, leaving ½-inch-thick shells. Place shells on lightly greased baking sheet.
6. To the skillet, add mashed mirliton pulp, parsley, thyme, and salt and pepper to taste. Cook another 5 minutes, then stir in all but 2 tablespoons of the bread crumbs and mix well.
7. Fill mirliton shells with the cooked mixture. Sprinkle with remaining bread crumbs and dot with remaining tablespoon butter.
8. Bake in upper third of oven 10 to 15 minutes, or until tops are lightly browned.
9. Remove from oven and, with wide metal spatula, place the stuffed mirlitons on individual serving plates. Serve at once.

Marinated Carrots

1 pound carrots
2 tablespoons finely sliced scallions, both green and white parts
2 tablespoons minced fresh parsley
¼ teaspoon oregano
Salt and freshly ground pepper
5 tablespoons olive oil
2 tablespoons red wine vinegar
Parsley sprigs for garnish (optional)

1. In large covered saucepan fitted with collapsible vegetable steamer, bring 1 inch of water to a boil.
2. Peel carrots and cut on diagonal into pieces 1 inch long and ½ inch wide. Steam 2 minutes, or until barely tender. Drain carrots in colander and turn into serving dish.
3. Trim and slice scallions, and mince parsley. Sprinkle carrots with scallions, parsley, oregano, and salt and pepper to taste.
4. Pour olive oil and vinegar over carrots. Toss lightly.
5. Allow carrots to marinate at least 15 minutes at room temperature before serving.
6. Serve carrots in the marinade and garnish with parsley sprigs, if desired.

Chicken Breasts with a Bouquet of Vegetables and Sweet-and-Sour Sauce
Green Salad with Herbed Vinaigrette

The cooking method for the chicken-and-vegetables entrée may seem complicated at first, yet it is systematic and an excellent technique to add to your repertoire. Using a large vegetable steamer with a wire basket, or a large covered saucepan with a colander, poach the leeks, cabbage leaves, garlic, and chicken breasts in apple cider. Simultaneously, steam the carrot slices, then the zucchini slices, in the basket or colander above the liquid, which you then cook down and use as the base for the sweet-and-sour sauce. Lightly steamed carrots and zuc-

Red cabbage leaves form individual "baskets" for the chicken and assorted vegetables. Serve the tart-sweet sauce for the main course in a pitcher or sauce boat, and the tossed green salad on separate plates.

chini retain their natural flavor and crunch. Because you add the ingredients in stages, nothing overcooks.

Beverly Cox calls for unsweetened apple cider, preferably filtered for a more translucent sauce. Avoid using a sweetened cider or a standard apple juice, both of which would produce an overly sweet sauce. If apple juice is your only option, choose one made from tart apples, such as McIntosh. After removing the chicken and vegetables from the liquid, add a good-quality, red wine vinegar and Dijon mustard, and cook until the seasoned cider thickens and becomes translucent.

The greens for the salad are sweet Bibb or Boston lettuce and slightly tart escarole. To select the greens, look for full, round heads of lettuce with crisp, unwilted leaves. Boston lettuce has pale-green leaves. Bibb, a

smaller, cup-shaped lettuce, has deep-green leaves. Before refrigerating, rinse the lettuce well in cold water, taking care not to bruise the leaves. Drain them well, and pat them as dry as possible. Wrap them in a clean dish towel and store in the refrigerator until dinnertime. Escarole, a variety of endive available all year, is a bushy green with broad leaves. Select and handle escarole just as you would lettuce.

WHAT TO DRINK

To accompany this medley of sweet and sharp tastes, you need a wine with its own concert of sweet and dry elements. A good Moselle of the Kabinett or Spatlese class would do very well, but perhaps the best complement to the main dish would be a good Washington State Riesling, which has a characteristic delicate apple aroma.

SHOPPING LIST AND STAPLES

2 whole skinless, boneless chicken breasts (about 1½ pounds total weight)
Small head red cabbage
6 medium-size carrots
3 medium-size zucchini
3 leeks
2 heads Boston or Bibb lettuce
Small head escarole
Fresh parsley sprigs (optional)
Fresh mint leaves

Fresh or frozen chives
3 cloves garlic
1½ quarts unsweetened apple cider
6 tablespoons peanut or safflower oil
3½ tablespoons red wine vinegar
1½ tablespoons Dijon mustard
Salt and freshly ground pepper

UTENSILS

Large steamer unit
  or covered saucepan large enough to hold a colander
2 small bowls
Colander (plus additional colander if not using steamer
  unit)
Measuring cups and spoons
Chef's knife
Paring knife
Slotted spoon
Whisk
Vegetable peeler
Salad spinner (optional)

START-TO-FINISH STEPS

1. Mince mint and garlic, snip chives, and follow green salad recipe step 1.
2. Follow chicken breasts recipe steps 1 through 4.
3. Follow green salad recipe step 2.
4. Clean salad greens, step 3.
5. Preheat oven to 200 degrees. Follow chicken breasts recipe steps 5 through 9.
6. Follow green salad recipe step 4, chicken breasts recipe step 10, and serve.

RECIPES

Chicken Breasts with a Bouquet of Vegetables and Sweet-and-Sour Sauce

6 cups unsweetened apple cider
3 leeks
Small head red cabbage
2 garlic cloves
2 whole skinless, boneless chicken breasts, halved (about
  1½ pounds total weight)
6 medium-size carrots

3 medium-size zucchini
1½ tablespoons red wine vinegar
1½ tablespoons Dijon mustard
Fresh parsley sprigs for garnish (optional)

1. Pour cider into bottom of large steamer unit or covered saucepan large enough to hold a colander. Bring to a boil.
2. Trim off root ends of leeks. Split lengthwise, gently spread leaves, and rinse well to remove any sand and grit. Cut each leek crosswise into ¼-inch slices. Trim cabbage of limp or darkened outer leaves, rinse, and remove 16 small leaves. Peel garlic.
3. Add leeks, cabbage leaves, and whole garlic to the cider. Reduce heat to a simmer and cook 5 minutes.
4. Halve chicken breasts, add to cider mixture, and return cider to a boil. Cover, reduce heat, and simmer 10 minutes.
5. Meanwhile, peel and trim carrots. Cut them into 2-inch lengths and cut each piece lengthwise into quarters. Place steamer basket or colander in pan. Add carrots, cover, and steam 3 minutes.
6. Wash and trim zucchini. Cut on diagonal into ½-inch ovals. Add to steamer basket and steam, covered, another 3 minutes. The vegetables should remain crisp.
7. Remove steamer basket or colander and with slotted spoon remove remaining vegetables and chicken from the poaching liquid. Discard garlic. Arrange cabbage, carrots, zucchini, and leeks in a decorative border on each dinner plate. Place 1 chicken breast half in center of each plate. Keep warm in oven.
8. Bring liquid to a boil, uncovered, and cook until reduced to one third the original amount, about 5 to 10 minutes. You should have about 2 cups.

Rinse leeks thoroughly to remove sand and grit.

9. Whisk vinegar and mustard into the reduced liquid and cook until it becomes syrupy and translucent, about 5 to 7 minutes.

10. Remove plates from oven. Spoon sauce over the chicken. Garnish with parsley, if desired, and serve at once.

Green Salad with Herbed Vinaigrette

1 tablespoon minced fresh mint
1½ teaspoons snipped chives, preferably fresh
½ teaspoon minced garlic
6 tablespoons peanut or safflower oil
2 tablespoons red wine vinegar
Salt and freshly ground pepper
2 heads Boston or Bibb lettuce
Small head escarole

1. In small bowl, marinate mint, chives, and garlic in oil 15 to 20 minutes.
2. Pour vinegar into another small bowl and gradually whisk in the oil and herbs. Season with salt and pepper to taste. Set aside.
3. Trim salad greens of any limp or browned outer leaves, root ends, and core. Wash well and dry in salad spinner or drain in colander and pat dry with paper towels. Wrap in kitchen towel and refrigerate until ready to use.
4. Just before serving, place greens in salad bowl and toss with the vinaigrette.

ADDED TOUCH

The surprise ingredient in this delicious cake is puréed beets. They not only tint the batter, but they add moisture as well.

Spicy Chocolate Beet Cake

4 sixteen-ounce cans beets, well drained
6 eggs
2½ cups granulated sugar
½ cup firmly packed dark brown sugar
1½ cups vegetable oil
3½ cups sifted all-purpose flour
4 teaspoons baking soda
½ teaspoon salt
¼ teaspoon ground cloves
¼ teaspoon cinnamon
5 ounces unsweetened baking chocolate

1¼ teaspoons vanilla extract
Chocolate glaze (see following recipe)

1. Preheat oven to 350 degrees.
2. Butter and flour 10-inch angel food cake pan or Bundt pan.
3. Drain beets well and purée them in food processor or blender. Set aside.
4. In large mixing bowl, beat eggs with hand mixer until pale yellow and frothy. Gradually beat in both the sugars and the oil, combining well.
5. Using spatula, fold beet purée into egg mixture.
6. Sift enough flour to measure 3½ cups onto a sheet of waxed paper, then sift baking soda, salt, cloves, and cinnamon into the flour and mix together well. Gradually fold dry ingredients into the beet mixture, making sure to combine well.
7. Melt chocolate in top of double boiler over simmering water. With spatula, fold chocolate and vanilla extract into the cake batter, continuing to mix gently until thoroughly incorporated.
8. Pour batter into prepared cake pan and bake in middle of oven 1½ hours, or until cake is firm to the touch and a toothpick or straw comes out clean when inserted in center of cake.
9. Invert cake onto baking rack and cool *completely* before frosting with chocolate glaze.

Chocolate Glaze

6 ounces semisweet baking chocolate
1 tablespoon unsalted butter
1 tablespoon light corn syrup
¾ cup heavy cream
Pinch of salt
½ teaspoon vanilla extract
Dash of cinnamon (optional)

1. Melt chocolate in top of double boiler.
2. Stir in butter and corn syrup, then gradually mix in cream. Continue to stir over simmering water until mixture is smooth and well blended, about 1 minute. Add salt, vanilla, and cinnamon, and stir again.
3. Set the thoroughly cooled cake still on its rack over a pan to catch any drippings and pour or drip the warm glaze over top of cake.
4. Lift rack and gently shake it to distribute the glaze evenly. Chill cake until glaze is set, about 20 to 30 minutes.

Jane Salzfass Freiman

MENU 1 (Left)
Seafood Salad
Cheese and Scallion Enchiladas
with Guacamole Sauce

MENU 2
Watercress Soup
Broiled Scrod with Red-Pepper Sauce
Steamed New Potatoes

MENU 3
Pasta with Fresh Mushroom Sauce
Boston Lettuce, Fennel, and Radicchio Salad

Because she grew up in California, where fruits and vegetables grow in abundance year round, Jane Salzfass Freiman says that fresh produce is integral to her menu planning. Now living in Chicago, she picks her own vegetables from her garden during the growing season, and, throughout the year, she serves at least one, sometimes two, fresh vegetable dishes each day—either a vegetable appetizer, often an Italian-style recipe, or a vegetable entrée and a salad, both in the same meal.

Through her cooking class and syndicated food column, Jane Salzfass Freiman promotes the use of fresh, natural ingredients of all kinds. Moreover, she creates recipes that stress strong, direct flavors, as in all three of the meals here. Menu 1 features two piquant Mexican-style courses, a seafood salad that is a modified version of *seviche,* in which fish requires overnight "cooking" in the acid of citrus-fruit juice. Her version speeds up the original recipe by quick-poaching the seafood and then marinating it in lime and orange juices. The accompanying enchiladas are covered with a guacamole spiked with fiery jalapeño chilies. Both the watercress soup and the red-pepper sauce for the broiled scrod of Menu 2 have assertive flavors that nonetheless balance each other. In Menu 3, she brings together a mildly seasoned pasta entrée with the fresh, powerful flavors of fennel and radicchio.

This Mexican-style meal features cheese-and-scallion-stuffed enchiladas and a chilled marinated seafood salad. When you serve the enchiladas, top each with a portion of the guacamole sauce and then with a spoonful of sour cream and a sliver of tomato. Sliced black olives and chopped coriander add color to the seafood salad.

47

Seafood Salad
Cheese and Scallion Enchiladas with Guacamole Sauce

This casual meal requires several Mexican ingredients, one of them corn tortillas for the main dish. Fresh corn tortillas, sealed in plastic bags, may be found in the dairy section of most supermarkets. If you buy paper-wrapped, fresh tortillas, remember that they dry out quickly, so store them in a tightly sealed plastic bag.

This guacamole sauce contains several unusual seasonings. Tomatillos—tart, green, and available year round—resemble tiny tomatoes. Fresh tomatillos have a paper-like skin that you peel away before cooking. Tomatillos are available at some supermarkets and at Mexican groceries. Select those that are yellow-green and do not have any bruises or discolorations. Canned tomatillos are on the gourmet shelves of well-stocked supermarkets and are acceptable substitutes. Coriander, also known as cilantro, or Chinese parsley, has a distinctive, earthy taste intrinsic to many Mexican and Oriental recipes. It has flat, pale-green leaves like Italian parsley; treat coriander as you would regular parsley. Fresh jalapeño peppers are readily available in many parts of the country, but you will find canned or pickled jalapeños at any supermarket that stocks Mexican ingredients. Handle jalapeño peppers with care. If possible, wear thin rubber gloves when you touch them; if you do handle them with your bare hands, be sure not to touch your eyes or mouth until you have washed your hands thoroughly with soap and water.

WHAT TO DRINK

To accompany these dishes, choose a crisp, fruity, dry white wine, such as an Italian Soave or Verdicchio, a California Chenin Blanc, or a French Vouvray.

SHOPPING LIST AND STAPLES

¼ pound shrimp, unshelled
¼-pound fresh scrod fillet or skinless red snapper fillet
¼ pound bay or sea scallops
1 large avocado (about ¾ pound)
1 large and 1 small ripe tomato
Small head lettuce
1 medium-size onion
7 fresh tomatillos (about ½ pound), or 13-ounce can
1 orange
1 lime
1 lemon
Small bunch scallions

Large bunch coriander
2 medium-size cloves garlic
3 tablespoons unsalted butter
½ pint sour cream
½ pound Monterey Jack cheese
1 package fresh corn tortillas, each 6 inches in diameter, or 9-ounce package frozen
4-ounce can jalapeño peppers
7-ounce can pitted black olives (optional)
1 tablespoon vegetable oil
Hot pepper sauce
Sugar
Salt

UTENSILS

Food processor or blender
Medium-size saucepan with cover
Small saucepan
Rectangular baking dish
Flat, glass baking dish
2 medium-size bowls
Colander
Strainer (if using canned tomatillos)
Measuring cups and spoons
Chef's knife
Paring knife
Wide, metal spatula
Slotted spoon
Wooden spoon
Rubber spatula
Cheese grater (if not using processor)
Salad spinner (optional)
Juicer (optional)
Pastry brush

START-TO-FINISH STEPS

At least 30 minutes ahead: If using frozen tortillas for enchiladas, remove from the freezer and unwrap.

1. Follow guacamole sauce recipe step 1.
2. Lightly rinse and pat dry scrod and scallops for seafood salad and follow recipe steps 1 through 3, using same saucepan used for cooking tomatillos.
3. Squeeze juices for seafood salad and for guacamole. Follow seafood salad recipe steps 4 and 5.
4. Prepare tortillas for enchiladas, steps 1 and 2.
5. Follow seafood salad recipe step 6.

6. Follow enchiladas recipe steps 3 through 6. Sliver tomato for garnish.

7. While enchiladas are baking, peel garlic, trim scallion, and dice jalapeño peppers for guacamole sauce. Follow steps 2 through 4.

8. Sliver olives and slice lime, if using for garnish, and complete seafood salad recipe, steps 7 and 8.

9. When enchiladas are baked, follow recipe step 7, and serve with the seafood salad.

RECIPES

Seafood Salad

Small bunch coriander
¼ pound shrimp, unshelled
¼-pound fresh scrod fillet or skinless red snapper fillet
¼ pound bay scallops, or sea scallops, cut into ¼-inch dice
½ medium onion
1 large ripe tomato
¼ cup fresh lime juice
⅓ cup fresh orange juice
¼ teaspoon salt
Pinch of sugar
Several dashes of hot pepper sauce
Small head lettuce
Black olives, slivered, for garnish (optional)

1. Immerse coriander in bowl of cold water to soak.

2. In covered medium-sized saucepan, bring 2 cups of water to a rolling boil. Add shrimp and cook briefly, about 2 minutes, or until they turn pink. Using slotted spoon, transfer shrimp to colander and refresh under cold running water. Add fish and scallops to the boiling water. Turn off heat, cover, and set aside 5 minutes.

3. Shell and devein shrimp. Cut into ¼-inch dice. Place in flat, glass baking dish.

4. Peel and cut onion into ⅛-inch dice; set aside. Core and cut tomato into ¼-inch dice. Add onion, tomato, lime juice, orange juice, salt, sugar, and hot pepper sauce to baking dish, and stir to combine. Refrigerate mixture.

5. Using slotted spoon, remove fish and scallops from pan, and drain in colander. Carefully check fish and discard any stray bones. With fork, separate fish fillet into flakes. While fish and scallops are still hot, add to dish in refrigerator and stir to combine.

6. Drain coriander and remove stems. Dry in salad spinner or pat dry with paper towels. Reserve ¼ cup firmly packed coriander for guacamole sauce. Wrap remainder in towel; refrigerate until ready to use.

7. Just before serving, mince 2 tablespoons of coriander and add to fish. Stir to combine; taste for seasoning.

8. Serve seafood salad on lettuce leaves, garnished with slivers of black olives, if desired.

Cheese and Scallion Enchiladas

8 corn tortillas, each about 6 inches in diameter
2 scallions
½ pound Monterey Jack cheese, chilled
3 tablespoons unsalted butter
Guacamole sauce (see following recipe)
4 heaping tablespoonfuls sour cream
1 small ripe tomato, slivered, for garnish

1. Adjust oven rack to middle position. Preheat oven to 425 degrees.

2. Stack tortillas and wrap in foil. Heat in oven until warm and flexible, about 6 to 8 minutes.

3. Trim scallions and slice into thin rings.

4. Using food processor or cheese grater, shred cheese.

5. In small saucepan, melt butter. Using pastry brush, brush rectangular baking dish with melted butter. Brush 1 side of each tortilla with melted butter, reserving a tablespoonful. Divide cheese evenly down center of tortillas, then sprinkle with scallions. Tightly roll tortillas and place them side by side in baking dish, folded side down. Gently press tortillas to help keep them from unfolding. Brush tops of tortillas with remaining butter and cover dish tightly with foil.

6. Bake 12 to 15 minutes, or until cheese melts. Remove from oven and loosen foil to allow steam to escape.

7. Using wide, metal spatula, place 2 enchiladas on each dinner plate. Cover each enchilada generously with guacamole sauce and garnish each with a heaping spoonful of sour cream and a tomato sliver. Serve immediately.

Guacamole Sauce

7 fresh tomatillos (about ½ pound) or 13-ounce can
2 medium-size cloves garlic, peeled
1 scallion, trimmed
¼ cup firmly packed fresh coriander
1½ teaspoons to 1 tablespoon diced, canned jalapeño peppers, according to taste
1 large avocado (about ¾ pound)
1 tablespoon fresh lemon juice
1 tablespoon vegetable oil
¾ teaspoon salt (approximately)

1. If using fresh tomatillos, remove and discard paper-like skins; rinse tomatillos. Place tomatillos in medium-size saucepan with cold water to cover. Cover pan, bring water to a boil, and cook 1 minute. Drain in colander, then place tomatillos in bowl of ice water. Set aside. If using canned tomatillos, simply drain in strainer, rinse, and set aside. (They are already cooked.)

2. Chop garlic, scallion, and coriander in food processor or blender. Add jalapeños and process until ingredients are minced. If using fresh tomatillos, first drain them in strainer. Then halve tomatillos and add them to processor. Process until puréed and well combined, scraping down sides of container with rubber spatula as necessary.

3. Halve avocado and remove pit. Peel and slice avocado, add to mixture, and process to combine well.

4. Add lemon juice, oil, and salt to taste. Process once more. Set sauce aside at room temperature until ready to serve enchiladas. Just before serving, taste again and adjust seasonings if necessary.

Watercress Soup
Broiled Scrod with Red-Pepper Sauce
Steamed New Potatoes

The colorful garnishes here will enhance this meal of watercress soup, scrod with red-pepper sauce, and new potatoes.

S crod is the name for cod, haddock, or pollack that weigh two pounds or less. These small, young fish are ideal for broiling because they retain their moisture and fine texture.

WHAT TO DRINK

The cook recommends a California Fumé Blanc or an Italian Pinot Grigio for this meal. A light red wine, such as a very young Zinfandel, is another possibility.

SHOPPING LIST AND STAPLES

1 to 1½ pounds skinned scrod fillets
1 pound small, new potatoes
1 baking potato (about ½ pound)
1 large red bell pepper
1 to 2 bunches watercress (about 6 ounces)
1 bunch scallions
1 medium-size shallot
½ cup milk

½ pint heavy cream
1 stick plus 2 tablespoons unsalted butter
3½ cups chicken stock, preferably homemade (see page 13), or canned
2 tablespoons olive or vegetable oil
1 tablespoon white wine vinegar
Hot pepper sauce
Salt and freshly ground white pepper
1½ cups dry white wine

UTENSILS

Food processor or blender
Large, heavy-gauge non-aluminum saucepan with cover
Large saucepan with cover
Medium-size saucepan
Broiler pan
Large mixing bowl
Medium-size bowl
Collapsible vegetable steamer
Colander

Strainer
Measuring cups and spoons
Chef's knife
Paring knife
Wide, metal spatula
2 wooden spoons
Rubber spatula
Vegetable peeler
Wire whisk
Soup ladle
Tweezers
Salad spinner (optional)

START-TO-FINISH STEPS

1. Trim root ends and leafy green tops from scallions. Cut each scallion into 1-inch lengths. Peel baking potato and cube. Follow watercress soup recipe steps 1 through 3.
2. Peel and slice shallot; rinse, core, seed, and cut red bell pepper into ½-inch squares; and with tweezers remove small bones from scrod fillets. Follow broiled scrod recipe steps 1 and 2.
3. Scrub new potatoes and follow recipe steps 1 and 2.
4. Follow soup recipe steps 4 through 7.
5. Follow scrod recipe steps 3 through 5.
6. Follow watercress soup recipe step 8 and serve.
7. Follow scrod recipe steps 6 through 8 and potatoes recipe step 3. Serve at once.

RECIPES

Watercress Soup

4 scallions, trimmed and cut into 1-inch lengths
1 baking potato (about ½ pound), peeled and cubed
3½ cups chicken stock
½ cup milk
1 to 2 bunches watercress (about 6 ounces)
¼ teaspoon salt
Twist of freshly ground white pepper
Several dashes hot pepper sauce
½ cup heavy cream

1. In food processor fitted with metal blade or in blender, chop scallions. With machine running, add potato cubes, and then in a slow, steady stream add 1 cup of the chicken stock. Process until potato is puréed.
2. Transfer purée to large, heavy-gauge non-aluminum saucepan. With wooden spoon, stir in remaining stock and milk. Cover and simmer about 15 minutes.
3. Wash watercress, discard stems, and drain leaves. Dry in salad spinner or pat dry with paper towels.
4. Put watercress, salt, pepper, and hot pepper sauce in processor bowl or blender (there is no need to wash it). Process until watercress is finely minced, scraping down sides of container with rubber spatula.
5. Bring purée-stock mixture to a simmer. Add half the cream in a slow, steady stream, stirring to combine.
6. Return liquid to a simmer. Add half the liquid to the watercress. Process about 1 minute. Empty into large mixing bowl. Add remaining liquid to processor. Process 30 seconds and add to mixture in bowl and stir to blend.
7. Wipe out saucepan with paper towels and return all the soup to it. Adjust seasonings to taste and keep covered until ready to serve.
8. Before serving, reheat soup, stirring occasionally, over low heat. Do not allow soup to boil. To serve, garnish each portion with a tablespoon of the remaining cream.

Broiled Scrod with Red-Pepper Sauce

1½ cups dry white wine
1 medium-size shallot, peeled and sliced
1 large red bell pepper
1 to 1½ pounds skinless scrod fillets, bones removed
2 tablespoons olive or vegetable oil
Salt
1 tablespoon white wine vinegar
1 stick plus 2 tablespoons unsalted butter
Freshly ground white pepper

1. In medium-size saucepan, combine white wine, shallot, and red pepper. Boil uncovered over high heat until no more than 2 tablespoons of liquid remain in pan, about 10 minutes. Remove from heat and set aside to cool slightly.
2. Rinse fish fillets and pat dry. Cut into 4 equal portions. Rub both sides with oil, and sprinkle lightly with salt.
3. Process red pepper and liquid in food processor or blender until smooth. Return mixture to saucepan. Using wooden spoon, stir in vinegar and about ¼ teaspoon salt. Add 1 stick butter, cut into pieces, whisking continuously over low heat until butter melts, about 5 minutes.
4. Place broiler rack 4 inches from heat source and pre-heat broiler pan.
5. Strain sauce over medium-size bowl, using a spoon to push it through mesh. Wipe the saucepan clean, pour strained sauce into it, and set aside.
6. Place scrod on hot broiler pan and broil 5 to 6 minutes, or until fish is opaque.
7. Meanwhile, turn heat to low under pepper sauce. Whisk in remaining 2 tablespoons of butter, in pieces. Taste; add salt and white pepper to taste. When sauce is heated through, spoon about ¼ cup onto each dinner plate.
8. When fish is done, remove immediately from broiler pan with wide, metal spatula. Place fish on sauce.

Steamed New Potatoes

1 pound small, new potatoes, peeled
Salt

1. If necessary, cut potatoes into uniform size.
2. In bottom of large saucepan fitted with vegetable steamer, bring 1 to 1½ inches of cold water to a boil. Add potatoes and sprinkle with salt. Cover and steam over high heat about 20 minutes, or until potatoes can be pierced easily with tip of small knife. Cover until ready to serve. Reheat if necessary.
3. When ready to serve, remove potatoes from steamer and arrange on dinner plates.

Pasta with Fresh Mushroom Sauce
Boston Lettuce, Fennel, and Radicchio Salad

Tomato-colored and plain linguine are topped with a sauce of sautéed mushrooms. Serve this dish family style or on individual dinner plates. The three-vegetable salad gains added substance from cheese cubes and ham strips.

For this Italian-style meal, Jane Salzfass Freiman brings together two effortless dishes: an uncomplicated pasta entrée and a mixed green salad. For the entrée, use either fettuccine or linguine; combine plain pasta with tomato-flavored pasta if you wish. Mushrooms are the primary ingredient for the lightly seasoned pasta sauce.

The crisp salad offsets the soft textures of the pasta and its sauce. The cook calls for two Italian vegetables: fennel and radicchio. The latter, a ruby-red chicory native to Treviso, Italy, has a slightly bitter but agreeable taste and classically is combined with fennel, which is slightly sweet. Radicchio has a limited winter season, so at other times of the year you can use the familiar red cabbage instead.

WHAT TO DRINK

Here, the classic choice would be a dry, fairly full-bodied white wine: a California Chardonnay or a French Chablis or young Muscadet.

SHOPPING LIST AND STAPLES

2 ounces good-quality boiled ham
1½ pounds mushrooms
Small bulb fennel with feathery top (about ½ pound)
Medium-size head Boston lettuce
Small head radicchio or small red cabbage
1 lemon
Small bunch parsley
3 medium-size cloves garlic
½ pound fresh linguine or fettuccine, or 1 pound total
    if not using tomato linguine or fettuccine
½ pound fresh tomato linguine or fettuccine
½ pint heavy cream
4 ounces mozzarella
¾ cup plus 3 tablespoons olive oil
2 tablespoons sherry vinegar or red wine vinegar
1½ teaspoons Dijon mustard
Salt and freshly ground pepper
½ cup dry white wine

UTENSILS

Food processor (optional)
Stockpot or kettle with cover

12-inch skillet
Salad bowl
Large bowl
Small bowl or jar
Colander
Measuring cups and spoons
Chef's knife
Paring knife
2 wooden spoons
Wooden spatula
Salad servers or 2 large forks
Salad spinner (optional)
Juicer (optional)

START-TO-FINISH STEPS

1. Follow pasta recipe step 1.
2. Core lettuce and radicchio, and follow salad recipe step 1.
3. Mince garlic, juice lemon, and mince parsley for pasta. Follow recipe steps 2 through 5.
4. Follow salad recipe steps 2 through 4. Preheat oven to 200 degrees and warm 4 dinner plates in oven.
5. Follow pasta recipe steps 6 through 8.
6. Toss salad, step 5. Remove plates from oven and follow pasta recipe step 9. Serve the salad on separate plates with the pasta.

RECIPES

Pasta with Fresh Mushroom Sauce

Salt
1½ pounds mushrooms
½ cup plus 3 tablespoons olive oil
2½ teaspoons minced garlic
½ cup dry white wine
2 teaspoons lemon juice
¼ teaspoon salt
¼ teaspoon freshly ground pepper
2 teaspoons minced parsley
½ pound fresh linguine or fettuccine, or 1 pound total if not using tomato linguine or fettuccine
½ pound fresh tomato linguine or fettuccine

1. In covered stockpot or kettle, bring 4 quarts lightly salted water to a boil.
2. Wipe mushrooms clean with damp paper towels. Slice thinly with chef's knife or in food processor fitted with slicing disc.
3. In 12-inch skillet, heat ¼ cup of the olive oil over medium heat. Add garlic and cook until garlic is fragrant, about 2 minutes. Add mushrooms, toss to coat with oil, and continue tossing until mushrooms exude their juices, about 5 minutes.
4. Add white wine, lemon juice, and salt. Bring to a simmer, and cook rapidly until liquid evaporates, about 15 minutes, stirring frequently with wooden spatula.
5. When liquid has evaporated, stir in ¼ cup olive oil,

pepper, and parsley. Taste for seasoning. The sauce should be slightly salty and peppery. Remove sauce from heat and set aside until pasta is cooked.
6. Add pasta to the boiling water and stir well to combine both pastas. Boil until noodles are tender but still firm, 2 to 4 minutes. Drain immediately in colander.
7. Heat remaining 3 tablespoons olive oil in pasta pot over low heat. Add noodles and using 2 wooden spoons, toss to coat. Continue tossing until any excess liquid evaporates and noodles begin to separate, 1 to 1½ minutes.
8. Reheat mushroom sauce over low heat.
9. Divide noodles among warm dinner plates. Top with sauce and serve immediately.

Boston Lettuce, Fennel, and Radicchio Salad

Medium-size head Boston lettuce, cored
Small head radicchio, cored, or 2-ounce wedge red cabbage
Small bulb fennel (about ½ pound)
4 ounces mozzarella
2 ounces good-quality boiled ham, julienned
2 tablespoons sherry vinegar or red wine vinegar
1½ teaspoons Dijon mustard
Salt and freshly ground pepper
1 tablespoon heavy cream
4 tablespoons olive or vegetable oil

1. Immerse lettuce, radicchio, and fennel in large bowl of cold water. Let stand 5 to 10 minutes, agitating several times to remove any dirt. Drain vegetables in colander and dry in salad spinner or pat dry with paper towels. Wrap vegetables in towel and refrigerate until ready to complete salad.
2. To assemble salad, separate lettuce leaves and tear into bite-size pieces; place leaves in salad bowl. Shred radicchio and add to bowl. Trim and discard fennel stalks; reserve feathery greens for use in salad dressing. Halve fennel bulb, then slice across grain; add fennel slices to bowl.
3. Dice enough mozzarella to make 1 cup and slice enough ham in julienne strips to make ½ cup. Add mozzarella and ham to salad. Cover with cloth towel and refrigerate until ready to serve.
4. Chop fennel greens to make 2 tablespoons. In small bowl or jar, combine vinegar, mustard, and salt and pepper to taste. Mix well with fork or shake jar. Add chopped fennel greens and cream, and mix until blended. Add oil in a slow, steady stream, mixing constantly. If using jar, shake vigorously to combine. Set aside at room temperature.
5. When ready to serve, pour dressing down side of salad bowl, allowing it to run to bottom. Using salad servers or 2 large forks, toss salad thoroughly.

ADDED TOUCH

Wash, hull, and quarter 2 pints of strawberries, then marinate briefly in Grand Marnier or another orange-flavored liqueur. Serve berries over vanilla ice cream.

Martha Rose Shulman

MENU 1 (Left)
Saffron Millet
Stir-Fried Tofu with Snow Peas
Hot-and-Sour Cucumber Salad

MENU 2
Chilies con Queso (Chilies with Cheese Fondue)
Spanish Rice
Guacamole Chalupas

MENU 3
Puffed Broccoli Omelets
Wild Rice with Almonds
Curried Pumpkin Purée

Martha Rose Shulman learned to appreciate exotic and sophisticated foods when, as a teenager, she traveled throughout Europe and Mexico with her family. In her early twenties, she became a vegetarian because, although she had no philosophical objections to eating meat, she preferred the nutritious, low-fat nature of a well-balanced meatless diet. She quickly discovered that there was plenty of culinary variety open to her. Now a professional cook, she has integrated her quest for good nutrition with her passion for good food. She has spent many years collecting vegetarian recipes from various national cuisines—enough to serve as the foundation for her "supper club" and catering business and two cookbooks. "Vegetarianism does not limit anyone's choice of foods," she says. "Instead, it gives the eager cook an assortment of recipes from every culture."

To prove her point, she offers three menus with international connections. Menu 1 combines several Asian ingredients (dried black mushrooms, fresh ginger, and tofu) that are stir fried and served over saffron-flavored millet—a grain dish similar to rice but a versatile and delicious alternative to it. Menu 2 is a compendium of Mexican dishes ranging from fiery to mild. Menu 3, which calls for wild rice and pumpkin, is distinctly American, although the omelet and curry powder echo other national cuisines as well.

Golden grains of saffron millet are the base for stir-fried tofu, snow peas, black mushrooms, and sliced scallions. The hot-and-sour sliced cucumber salad provides a strong contrast in flavor.

Saffron Millet
Stir-Fried Tofu with Snow Peas
Hot-and-Sour Cucumber Salad

I n this light, nonseasonal dinner, the entrée is stir-fried tofu and vegetables served with millet, a coarse-ground grain with a nutty flavor. You can buy millet by the pound in health-food stores, which usually stock it loose. Like rice and other cereals, millet must be boiled, but sautéing it first, as you do in this recipe, cuts down the time needed for boiling.

Saffron, which colors and flavors the millet, is a pungent and expensive spice that comes from the crocus blossom. Fortunately, a little goes a long way: half a teaspoon is plenty for this dish. Shop for saffron in specialty shops or good supermarkets. If you prefer, substitute turmeric, which is more economical and readily available. It has a musky flavor that will change the taste of the millet dish, but will give it the same golden color achieved by the use of saffron.

Tofu, or soybean curd, a ubiquitous ingredient in all Asian cooking, comes in a wide range of textures. For stir frying, buy the firm, Chinese-style variety because it holds its shape. It is a good source of protein and, because it is bland, lends itself to a variety of combinations with other ingredients. Most supermarkets routinely carry it, usually as a dairy item. Refrigerate unused tofu in water in a sealed container. If you change the water daily, tofu will stay fresh a week to 10 days.

The dried mushrooms for the main dish must be softened in water before you add them to other ingredients. Chinese groceries and specialty food shops sell them in 4-ounce or 8-ounce plastic or cellophane packages. Wrapped airtight, they last indefinitely. They are excellent in almost any stir-fried dish.

Snow peas should be available at the greengrocer or supermarket year round. Select unblemished, crisp-looking green pods. They will keep a day in a plastic bag in the refrigerator. To string the pods, pinch the stem top and pull the string off along with it. If you can find sugar snap peas, they make a good substitute.

A spoonful of Pernod, the licorice-flavored French aperitif, adds an unexpected but compatible flavor to the sauce in the main dish. You can substitute any anise-flavored liqueur or omit it altogether.

Tamari, which both the tofu and the salad recipe call for, is a strong Japanese soy sauce with a deep rich taste. You can find it in health-food stores.

Either a dessert soufflé or a fruit sherbet would provide a refreshing contrast to the highly seasoned, crunchy dishes in this menu.

WHAT TO DRINK

The cook suggests a medium-dry white wine for this meal. A German or domestic Riesling would be a good choice.

SHOPPING LIST AND STAPLES

1 pound fresh tofu
½ pound snow peas, or 1 bunch broccoli
2 large cucumbers
1 bunch scallions
1 lemon
1 clove garlic
Fresh ginger
2½ cups vegetable stock, preferably homemade
   (see page 13), optional
7 tablespoons safflower oil
2 tablespoons Oriental sesame oil
3 tablespoons white wine vinegar or apple cider vinegar
4 tablespoons soy sauce, preferably tamari
1 tablespoon plus 1 teaspoon mild-flavored honey, such as
   acacia, clover, or lavender
1 cup millet
1 tablespoon cornstarch or arrowroot
8 small or 4 large dried Chinese black mushrooms
   (about 1 ounce)
½ teaspoon crushed saffron threads or ground turmeric
⅛ to ¼ teaspoon Cayenne pepper, or ½ teaspoon hot
   pepper flakes
Salt
Freshly ground black pepper
1 tablespoon dry sherry
1 teaspoon Pernod or other anise-flavored liqueur

UTENSILS

Wok or large, heavy-gauge skillet with cover
Medium-size, heavy-gauge saucepan with cover
Small saucepan
Teakettle
Salad bowl
3 small bowls plus 1 bowl (if not using mortar and pestle)
Strainer
Measuring cups and spoons
Chef's knife
Paring knife
Chinese metal wok spatula or wooden spoon

Mortar and pestle (optional)
Vegetable peeler (optional)
Cheesecloth (optional)

START-TO-FINISH STEPS

1. Follow millet recipe step 1, squeeze enough lemon to measure 1 tablespoon juice, crush saffron threads, if using, in mortar with pestle or in small bowl with back of spoon, and follow step 2.
2. Bring water to a boil in teakettle and follow stir-fried tofu recipe step 1.
3. For tofu recipe, string snow peas or, if using broccoli, rinse, trim stems, and break broccoli into flowerets. Trim off scallion roots and any limp green tops; then cut into 1-inch lengths. Peel and mince garlic clove and enough ginger to measure 2 teaspoons. Cube tofu.
4. Follow tofu recipe steps 2 and 3.
5. Prepare cucumber salad, steps 1 and 2.
6. Follow tofu recipe steps 4 and 5.
7. Remove millet from heat and follow step 3. Follow tofu recipe step 6 and serve with the cucumber salad.

RECIPES

Saffron Millet

2½ cups vegetable stock or water
2 tablespoons safflower oil
1 cup millet
½ teaspoon crushed saffron threads or ground turmeric
¼ teaspoon salt
1 tablespoon lemon juice

1. In small saucepan, bring stock or water to a boil.
2. In medium-size, heavy-gauge saucepan, heat oil over medium heat and sauté millet about 2 minutes, until it begins to smell toasty. Pour in stock or water and bring to a boil. Stir in saffron or turmeric, salt, and lemon juice. Reduce heat, cover, and cook 35 to 40 minutes, or until liquid is absorbed. Keep covered until ready to serve.
3. Arrange millet along sides of serving platter, leaving room in middle for tofu-vegetable mixture.

Stir-Fried Tofu with Snow Peas

8 small or 4 large dried Chinese black mushrooms
2 cups snow peas, strings removed, or broccoli flowerets
3 scallions, cut into 1-inch lengths
¾ pound fresh tofu, cut into 1-inch cubes

The sauce:
1 tablespoon cornstarch or arrowroot
¼ cup water
1 tablespoon dry sherry
1 tablespoon Oriental sesame oil
1 teaspoon honey
1 teaspoon Pernod or other anise-flavored liqueur
2 tablespoons soy sauce, preferably tamari

2 tablespoons safflower oil
1 clove garlic, minced
2 teaspoons finely minced fresh ginger

1 tablespoon soy sauce, preferably tamari

1. Place mushrooms in small bowl and cover with boiling water. Let stand 20 to 30 minutes, or until soft.
2. Arrange remaining vegetables and tofu in piles on large cutting board or place on separate plates.
3. In small bowl, combine sauce ingredients and set aside.
4. When mushrooms have softened, remove from soaking liquid and rinse with cold water to dislodge any grit trapped in gills. Squeeze out excess liquid and reserve. Remove tough stems and cut mushrooms into strips. Over small bowl, pour soaking liquid through strainer lined with cheesecloth or paper towels and reserve.
5. In wok or large, heavy-gauge skillet, heat safflower oil over medium heat until hot. Add garlic and ginger, and sauté, stirring with wooden spoon or Chinese metal wok spatula, 10 seconds. Add tofu and soy sauce, and stir fry 1 minute. Add mushrooms and snow peas or broccoli and stir fry another 1 to 2 minutes. Pour in reserved mushroom liquid, cover, and simmer 3 to 5 minutes, or until vegetables are crisp-tender. Add scallions. Stir sauce mixture, making sure cornstarch is dissolved, and add to the vegetables. Cook, stirring, until sauce thickens and glazes the vegetables.
6. Remove from heat and mound mixture in middle of serving platter surrounded by saffron millet.

Hot and Sour Cucumber Salad

3 tablespoons white wine vinegar or apple cider vinegar
1 tablespoon mild-flavored honey, such as acacia, clover, or lavender
1 tablespoon soy sauce, preferably tamari
⅛ to ¼ teaspoon Cayenne pepper, or ½ teaspoon hot pepper flakes
¼ teaspoon freshly ground pepper
3 tablespoons safflower oil
1 tablespoon Oriental sesame oil
2 large cucumbers
2 tablespoons minced scallions

1. To prepare dressing, combine all ingredients in salad bowl except cucumbers and scallions. Stir well to combine.
2. Peel cucumbers and slice very thinly. Toss cucumbers with dressing and minced scallions. Cover and refrigerate until ready to serve.

LEFTOVER SUGGESTIONS

Since you use only three quarters of the pound block of tofu, you will have some left over. Add it to omelets, scrambled eggs, soups, salads, or stir-fried rice. Add vegetables, diced meat, or even fruit and nuts to leftover millet for another stir-fried meal.

Chilies con Queso (Chilies with Cheese Fondue)
Spanish Rice
Guacamole Chalupas

Chilies con queso, *a Mexican-style cheese fondue, is eaten with a variety of dippers: carrots, zucchini, red peppers and tostada chips. The hearty side dishes are Spanish rice and* chalupas, *a salad layered on crisp tortillas.*

T he main dish here is melted cheese spiked with hot chilies and flavored with onion, tomatoes, and beer—a lively Mexican version of a Swiss fondue. *Chalupas,* "little boats," are crisp corn tortillas filled with salad. Canned green *jalapeño* and *serrano* chilies are easy to find in supermarkets that carry Mexican ingredients, but *chipotles* may be available only at Mexican groceries.

WHAT TO DRINK

For this menu, choose a dark Mexican beer or a simple Côtes du Rhône or California Zinfandel.

SHOPPING LIST AND STAPLES

7 medium-size ripe tomatoes
3 small or 2 large ripe avocados, preferably the dark, knobby Haas variety
2 medium-size carrots
1 red plus 3 green bell peppers
1 medium-size zucchini
1 small plus 1 medium-size onion
1 lemon
3-ounce package alfalfa sprouts
1 bunch cilantro
4 cloves garlic
1 pint plain, low-fat yogurt
½ pound Gruyère cheese
¼ pound Cheddar cheese
8 fresh corn tortillas, or 9-ounce package frozen
2 cups chicken or vegetable stock, preferably homemade (see page 13), or canned
7-ounce can whole jalapeño or chipotle peppers
3-ounce can serrano peppers, or 7-ounce can jalapeños
3 tablespoons safflower oil (approximately)
1 tablespoon vinegar
Tostada chips
1 cup long-grain rice
1 tablespoon cornstarch
1 ounce shelled sunflower seeds (optional)
Ground cumin
Chili powder
½ teaspoon crushed saffron threads or ground turmeric
Salt and freshly ground pepper
12-ounce bottle beer
½ cup dry white wine

Food processor (optional)
10-inch skillet
Large, heavy-bottomed sauté pan
Medium-size saucepan
Small saucepan
Chafing dish or fondue pot
2 medium-size serving bowls
Small bowl (if not using mortar and pestle)
Colander
Measuring cups and spoons
Chef's knife
Paring knife
2 wooden spoons
Tongs
Vegetable peeler
Cheese grater (if not using processor)
Mortar and pestle (optional)

START-TO-FINISH STEPS

At least 30 minutes ahead: If using frozen tortillas for chalupas, remove from the freezer and unwrap. Do not try to separate still-frozen tortillas.

1. Prepare the vegetables for all three recipes.
2. Follow chilies con queso recipe steps 1 though 4.
3. Follow Spanish rice recipe steps 1 through 6.
4. While rice is cooking, juice lemon, grate cheese for chilies and for chalupas in food processor fitted with grating disc or with cheese grater, and follow chalupas recipe steps 1 through 3. Preheat oven to 200 degrees.
5. Follow chilies con queso recipe step 5.

6. Follow chalupas recipe step 4.
7. Turn rice into serving bowl. Follow chilies con queso recipe step 6, chalupas recipe step 5, and serve with the rice.

RECIPES

Chilies con Queso

1 medium-size zucchini, sliced lengthwise into spears
3 canned whole jalapeño or chipotle peppers
1 tablespoon cornstarch
2 tablespoons beer or water
1 tablespoon safflower oil
½ medium-size onion, chopped
1 clove garlic, minced
2 ripe tomatoes, peeled, seeded, and chopped
½ cup beer
2 cups grated Gruyère cheese (about ½ pound)
2 carrots, scraped and sliced lengthwise into spears
2 green bell peppers, cored, seeded, and sliced lengthwise into thick strips
½ red bell pepper, cored, seeded, and sliced lengthwise into thick strips
Tostada chips

1. In medium-size saucepan, bring 3 cups of water to a boil. Add zucchini and blanch 1 minute. Drain in colander and refresh under cold running water. Wrap in paper towels and refrigerate until ready to serve.
2. Seed and slice jalapeño or chipotle peppers. (*Note:* The capsaicin in the pepper veins and seeds can be extremely irritating to eyes and lips, so wash hands thoroughly immediately after handling peppers.)

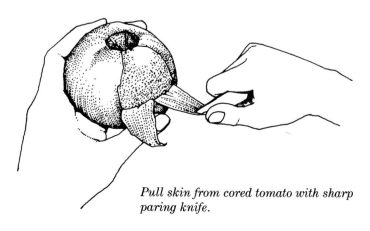

Pull skin from cored tomato with sharp paring knife.

Squeeze seeds out with one hand.

3. Dissolve cornstarch in 2 tablespoons of beer or water.
4. In same saucepan used for zucchini, heat oil over medium heat. Add onion and garlic, and sauté until onion is translucent. Add jalapeño peppers and tomatoes, stir, and cook 2 minutes over medium heat.
5. Add ½ cup beer to the tomato mixture and bring to a simmer. Slowly add cheese by handfuls, stirring until melted. Then gradually add cornstarch mixture, stirring until sauce is thick and smooth. Transfer sauce con queso to chafing dish or fondue pot and keep hot over low flame.
6. Remove zucchini from refrigerator. Arrange zucchini, carrots, peppers, and tostada chips on platter, ready for dipping into hot cheese sauce.

Spanish Rice

2 cups chicken or vegetable stock
1 to 2 tablespoons safflower oil
½ medium-size onion, chopped
2 cloves garlic, minced
½ green bell pepper, cored, seeded, and sliced lengthwise into strips
½ red bell pepper, cored, seeded, and sliced lengthwise into strips
2 ripe tomatoes, peeled, seeded, and chopped
1 cup long-grain rice
½ cup dry white wine
½ teaspoon crushed saffron threads or ground turmeric
Salt
Freshly ground pepper

1. In small saucepan, bring stock to a simmer.
2. In large, heavy-bottomed sauté pan, heat safflower oil over medium heat and sauté onion and garlic until onion begins to soften, about 2 minutes.
3. Add peppers and tomatoes to onion and garlic mixture, and sauté 2 minutes.
4. Add rice and sauté, stirring, about 2 minutes, or until rice is thoroughly coated with oil.
5. Add wine and cook, stirring, until wine has almost evaporated.
6. Crush saffron threads, if using, in mortar with pestle or in small bowl with back of spoon. Add saffron or turmeric and hot stock to pan, stir, and simmer, uncovered, over medium-low heat 20 to 25 minutes, or until liquid is absorbed and rice is *al dente*, slightly firm to the bite. Season with salt and freshly ground pepper to taste, and keep covered until ready to serve.

Guacamole Chalupas

1 to 2 canned serrano or jalapeño peppers
3 small or 2 large ripe avocados, preferably the dark, knobby Haas variety
3 ripe tomatoes, peeled, seeded, and chopped
1 small onion, minced
1 clove garlic, minced
Juice of ½ to 1 lemon
Salt
Ground cumin
Chili powder
2 to 3 tablespoons chopped cilantro
1 tablespoon vinegar
Safflower oil
8 corn tortillas, fresh or frozen
¼ pound Cheddar cheese, grated
1 pint plain, low-fat yogurt
1 cup alfalfa sprouts
¼ cup shelled sunflower seeds (optional)

1. Seed, devein, and chop peppers. (*Note:* The capsaicin in the pepper veins and seeds can be extremely irritating to eyes and lips, so wash hands thoroughly immediately after handling peppers.)
2. Cut avocados in half, remove pits, and scoop flesh out into medium-size serving bowl. Mash together avocados, one third of the chopped tomatoes, 2 tablespoons of the minced onion, and garlic. Season guacamole to taste with lemon juice, salt, cumin, and chili powder. Cover and refrigerate until ready to serve.
3. In another medium-size serving bowl, toss remaining chopped tomatoes and onion with chopped hot peppers, chopped cilantro, vinegar, and salt to taste. Cover and refrigerate. Line a heatproof platter with a triple layer of paper towels.
4. Add just enough oil to 10-inch skillet to coat bottom. Heat the oil over medium heat until hot. Add 1 tortilla and cook about 20 to 30 seconds on 1 side. Using tongs, carefully turn tortilla and cook another 20 to 30 seconds on the other side, or just until golden and crisp. Transfer to paper-towel-lined platter to drain. Repeat with remaining tortillas, adding more oil as necessary. Keep tortillas warm in oven until ready to serve.
5. Remove tortillas from oven and serve on a platter with the guacamole, tomato sauce, cheese, yogurt, sprouts, and sunflower seeds. Or serve tortillas plain, and let guests assemble their own combinations.

Puffed Broccoli Omelets
Wild Rice with Almonds
Curried Pumpkin Purée

Puffy golden broccoli omelets are accompanied by a curried pumpkin casserole and wild rice.

The grain dish in this meal, an ideal brunch for guests, is wild rice. The seeds of a wild grass, wild rice is harvested by hand. Hence, it is always in short supply and always expensive. However, one cup of wild rice will serve four. Good supermarkets and specialty food stores sell it in boxes. Adding almonds, onion, and sherry, as in this recipe, greatly enhances its earthy flavor.

Omelets are so easy to make and so versatile that they appear, in some form, in almost every national cuisine. Almost any vegetable, meat, or cheese filling is good with an omelet. The trick is to keep the eggs from sticking to the pan, so that you can fold them over the filling. Use a

nonstick skillet, as in this recipe, or a well-seasoned pan that you use only for omelets and scrambled eggs. Never allow it to overheat. For puffed omelets, which look like soufflés and take two minutes to make, beat the whites and yolks separately. The whites must be stiff and the yolks thick and pale.

If you use fresh pumpkin for the purée, buy a 2-pound pumpkin that is bright orange and feels heavy for its size. You can substitute two 16-ounce cans of pumpkin, if you wish. (Do *not* use pumpkin filling.) You can also use other winter squashes, such as butternut or acorn. Handle them the same way.

An uncomplicated wine would be the best choice here. If you want red, select a simple California Gamay; if you prefer white, choose an Italian Pinot Bianco or Pinot Grigio.

SHOPPING LIST AND STAPLES

2-pound pumpkin
1 bunch broccoli
Small onion
1 clove garlic
Fresh ginger, or ¼ teaspoon ground
6 eggs
5 tablespoons unsalted butter plus 2 tablespoons
    (if not using safflower oil)
½ pint plain low-fat yogurt, crème fraîche, or sour cream
¼ pound Parmesan cheese (optional)
2 cups vegetable or chicken stock
    preferably homemade (see page 13)
    or canned (optional)
2 tablespoons safflower oil (if not using butter)
1 tablespoon soy sauce
1 cup wild rice
3½-ounce package whole almonds
2 teaspoons curry powder
Salt and freshly ground pepper
2 tablespoons dry sherry

UTENSILS

Food processor or food mill
9- or 10-inch nonstick skillet
Large sauté pan
3 medium-size saucepans with covers
Baking sheet
Large bowl
2 medium-size bowls
Colander
Collapsible vegetable steamer
Measuring cups and spoons
Chef's knife
Paring knife
2 wooden spoons
Plastic spatula
Rubber spatula

Electric hand mixer
Cheese grater (optional)

START-TO-FINISH STEPS

One hour before meal: Remove eggs from refrigerator.

1. Wash rice in colander and follow wild rice recipe step 1.
2. As rice simmers, follow pumpkin purée recipe step 1.
3. Follow broccoli omelets recipe steps 1 and 2, using same saucepan and steamer used for pumpkin.
4. Slice enough almonds to measure 1 tablespoon and coarsely chop enough almonds to measure ⅓ cup. Follow rice recipe step 2. Reduce oven temperature to 200 degrees.
5. Grate fresh ginger, if using, and follow pumpkin purée recipe steps 2 through 4.
6. Grate cheese for omelets. Dice onion and chop almonds, and mince garlic for wild rice. Follow rice recipe steps 3 and 4.
7. Prepare omelets, steps 3 through 6. Serve with pumpkin purée and wild rice.

RECIPES

Puffed Broccoli Omelets

6 eggs, at room temperature
1 bunch broccoli
Salt and freshly ground pepper
¼ cup freshly grated Parmesan cheese (optional)
4 tablespoons unsalted butter

1. Separate eggs, dividing yolks between 2 medium-size bowls and placing all the whites in 1 large bowl.
2. Wash and trim broccoli and separate enough into flowerets to measure 2 cups. In saucepan fitted with vegetable steamer, steam the flowerets over 1 inch of water 10 minutes. Drain in colander. Chop half the flowerets; set aside the remainder.
3. Beat whites until stiff but not dry.
4. Beat 3 yolks and add salt and freshly ground pepper to taste. Using rubber spatula, gently fold in one third of whites, then fold in half the remaining whites, half the chopped broccoli, and 2 tablespoons of the cheese, if using.
5. In 9- or 10-inch nonstick skillet, heat 2 tablespoons of the butter over medium heat. When butter has sizzled, gently pour in egg mixture. Tilt pan to distribute mixture evenly and cook 1 minute. Arrange half the whole flower-

ets on one side of the omelet and cook omelet 1 more minute. With plastic spatula, carefully fold omelet over broccoli-lined half as you turn it out onto platter.

6. Follow steps 4 and 5 for preparing second omelet. Turn onto platter, beside first omelet. Serve at once.

Wild Rice with Almonds

2 cups vegetable or chicken stock, or water
1 cup wild rice, washed
1 tablespoon sliced almonds for garnish (optional)
2 tablespoons safflower oil or butter, or 1 tablespoon each
Small onion, diced
1 clove garlic, minced
⅓ cup coarsely chopped almonds

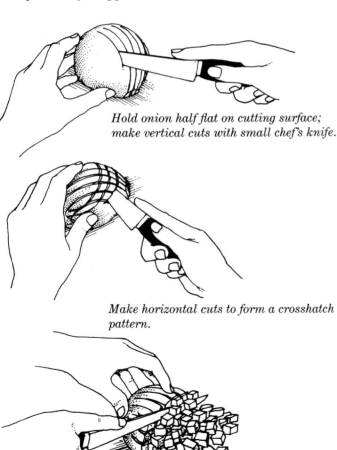

Hold onion half flat on cutting surface; make vertical cuts with small chef's knife.

Make horizontal cuts to form a crosshatch pattern.

Slice perpendicularly to cutting surface; onion will fall into dice.

2 tablespoons dry sherry
1 tablespoon soy sauce

1. In medium-size saucepan, bring stock or water to a boil and slowly stir in wild rice. Return to a boil. Reduce heat, cover, and simmer 45 minutes, or until tender and liquid is absorbed. Keep covered until ready to use.
2. Preheat oven to 400 degrees. Place sliced almonds on baking sheet and toast in oven about 3 to 5 minutes, or until golden. Set aside.
3. In large sauté pan, heat 1 tablespoon of the oil or butter over medium heat and sauté onion and garlic until onion is translucent. Add chopped almonds and sauté 1 minute.
4. Add remaining oil or butter and stir in cooked wild rice. Cook, stirring, 1 to 2 minutes. Add sherry and soy sauce. Toss rice over medium heat 1 to 2 minutes. Transfer to serving dish, garnish with toasted sliced almonds, and keep warm in oven until ready to serve.

Curried Pumpkin Purée

2-pound pumpkin
1 tablespoon unsalted butter
½ teaspoon grated fresh ginger, or ¼ teaspoon ground ginger
1½ to 2 teaspoons curry powder
2 tablespoons plain yogurt, crème fraîche, or sour cream
Salt
Freshly ground pepper

1. Quarter, seed, and peel pumpkin. Cut into small cubes. You will need about 4 cups. In saucepan fitted with steamer, steam pumpkin 15 minutes, or until tender. Drain in colander.
2. Purée pumpkin in food processor or put through food mill.
3. In another saucepan, melt butter. Add ginger and curry powder, and sauté, stirring, over low heat, 2 to 3 minutes.
4. Add pumpkin, yogurt, and salt and pepper to taste to mixture in saucepan, and stir to combine. Transfer to serving dish, cover loosely with foil, and keep warm in oven until ready to serve.

ADDED TOUCH

Fresh fruit is a satisfying dessert with this meal—try sliced pears, apples, or bananas, raw or poached. A dried-fruit compote also would complement this menu.

Peter Kump

MENU 1 (Right)
Fresh Beet Salad
Tomato and Onion Salad
Carrot and Horseradish Salad
Turkey Scallops with Brown Butter
and Caper Sauce
Green Beans with Sweet-and-Sour Sauce

MENU 2
Celeriac Winter Salad
Chicken Piccata
Braised Fresh Spinach and Mushrooms

MENU 3
Cream of Lemon Soup
Fillets of Sole with Zucchini and Peppers
Blueberry Cream-Cheese Parfaits

Austrians have always loved good food, particularly elaborate pastries. At the turn of the century, Viennese cooks could match their French counterparts dish for dish, but when the Empire collapsed, interest in elaborate recipes declined. Today, Austrian cooking is enjoying a renaissance.

Because Peter Kump is of Austrian descent, he has been especially curious about that country's food and has traveled there often to learn how to prepare authentic dishes. At his cooking school, he teaches Austrian techniques and recreates fine Old Empire dishes for his friends.

Menu 1 is a sampling of what an Austrian family might plan for an autumn dinner. Unlike the French, Austrians often serve several small salads to lighten otherwise rich, heavy meals, changing salad ingredients seasonally. Peter Kump mixes grated raw beets with minced onion, sour cream, and caraway seeds; thinly sliced tomatoes with a sprinkling of minced onions (the vinaigrette tenderizes the onions); and grated carrots with grated horseradish, a very important Austrian seasoning. The turkey scallops are dipped in beaten eggs and bread crumbs, sautéed, then served with a brown butter and caper sauce.

Vegetables are among Peter Kump's favorite ingredients. In Menu 2, he uses celeriac, a popular European root vegetable, and serves it in a salad with apples. In Menu 3, he serves fish fillets with grated zucchini, sliced, roasted red peppers, and minced shallots.

Three colorful vegetable salads—grated fresh beets, sliced tomatoes with minced onions, and grated carrots and horseradish—are unusual accompaniments to this Austrian-influenced meal. Present the turkey scallops and the green beans on the same platter.

Celeriac Winter Salad
Chicken Piccata
Braised Fresh Spinach and Mushrooms

Celeriac and apple salad, together with mushrooms braised lightly with spinach, provide interesting color and texture next to chicken piccata—sautéed chicken cutlets—garnished here with lemon slices and parsley sprigs.

This winter meal starts off with a sweet-and-sour salad of raw apples and celeriac—celery root—either grated or cut into fine julienne strips and marinated in a tenderizing homemade mayonnaise. Whole fresh celeriac looks lumpy and bewhiskered, but it tastes like a very flavorful celery and combines well with other raw vegetables. Good greengrocers and many supermarkets now stock celeriac. Buy roots that are no larger than 4 inches in diameter—otherwise the flesh may be woody. To prepare celeriac, remove the roots and leafy tops and scrub the tough outer skin. Then, with a paring knife, peel off the skin as if you were peeling citrus fruit. Since its skin is very thick you will need to trim away almost half the root. To prevent the flesh from darkening when exposed to air, sprinkle it with lemon juice, as Peter Kump suggests. You can use regular celery when celeriac is out of season.

For the braised spinach and mushrooms, coarsely chop the spinach leaves before cooking. This will make the spinach easier to eat.

WHAT TO DRINK

A full-bodied, dry white wine with plenty of character is in order here: a California Chardonnay or Sauvignon Blanc. The next best choice would be a very light red, perhaps a Beaujolais Nouveau.

SHOPPING LIST AND STAPLES

2 whole skinless, boneless chicken breasts
1½ pounds spinach
½ pound mushrooms
1 red apple, preferably Delicious
1 green apple
4 lemons plus 1 for garnish (optional)
1 small knob celeriac
1 medium-size onion
Curly parsley sprigs (optional)
1 large egg
1 stick plus 1 tablespoon unsalted butter
1 cup chicken stock, preferably homemade (see page 13),
    or canned
1 cup vegetable oil, preferably safflower
2 tablespoons Dijon mustard
½ cup slivered almonds
Whole nutmeg
Salt
Freshly ground pepper

UTENSILS

Food processor (optional)
Large sauté pan
Ovenproof casserole with cover
Baking sheet
Heatproof serving platter
2 serving bowls
2 large bowls
2 small bowls
Small cup
Colander
Measuring cups and spoons
Chef's knife
Paring knife
Slotted metal spoon
2 wooden spoons
Slotted metal spatula
Wooden spatula
Rubber spatula
Grater (if not using processor)
Nutmeg grater
Vegetable peeler
Whisk (if not using processor)

START-TO-FINISH STEPS

1. Preheat oven to 400 degrees.
2. Squeeze 2 lemons into small bowl to make 4 tablespoons juice and follow celeriac salad recipe steps 1 through 3.
3. Follow braised spinach recipe steps 1 and 2.
4. Follow celeriac salad recipe steps 4 and 5.
5. Follow spinach recipe steps 3 and 4, and grate nutmeg.
6. Follow chicken piccata recipe steps 1 and 2. Squeeze 1 lemon into small cup; slice the other thinly for garnish. Place serving dish and platter in oven to warm briefly.
7. Follow chicken recipe steps 3 through 5, spinach recipe step 5, celeriac salad recipe step 6, and serve.

RECIPES

Celeriac Winter Salad

1 small knob celeriac
Salt
4 tablespoons lemon juice
1 red apple, preferably Delicious
1 green apple

½ cup slivered almonds
1 large egg
2 tablespoons Dijon mustard
Freshly ground pepper
1 cup vegetable oil, preferably safflower

1. Peel celeriac, cut into thin slices, and then into fine julienne strips. Or, grate in food processor fitted with metal blade. Place celeriac in small bowl and sprinkle with 2 teaspoons salt and 2 tablespoons of lemon juice; set aside.

2. Core and quarter apples, but do not peel them. Cut them into fine julienne strips, or grate them in food processor or by hand. Wrap in damp cloth and refrigerate until ready to use.

3. Place almonds on baking sheet and toast in preheated oven about 3 to 4 minutes, or until golden. Remove from oven and set almonds aside until ready to use. Set oven at 325 degrees.

4. If using food processor, wipe clean. Combine egg (if making mayonnaise by hand, use only the yolk), mustard, remaining lemon juice, pinch of salt, and freshly ground pepper to taste in processor or large bowl. With processor running slowly or while whisking vigorously with wire whisk, add oil in a slow, steady stream until mayonnaise thickens and holds together.

5. Rinse celery root in colander to remove salt and pat dry with paper towels. Transfer to serving bowl, add the mustard-mayonnaise and toss well. Set aside. The longer the celeriac sits in the mayonnaise, the more it will tenderize.

6. Stir in the julienned or grated apple and the almonds, and serve.

Chicken Piccata

2 whole skinless, boneless chicken breasts
4 tablespoons unsalted butter
½ cup chicken stock
2 lemons, 1 freshly squeezed and 1 sliced for garnish
   (optional)
Salt
Freshly ground pepper
Sprigs of curly parsley for garnish (optional)

1. Halve chicken breasts and remove small mignon from underside of each of the 4 pieces. The mignon is about 1 inch wide at its widest point and about 4 inches long. Simply pull them from the breast halves; set aside.

2. Place the larger pieces of chicken on a cutting board and, with a chef's knife, cut each piece in half horizontally. You will end up with 8 cutlets and 4 mignons.

3. In sauté pan large enough to hold all the chicken in a single layer (or you can cook them in 2 batches) heat 2 tablespoons of the butter over medium heat. While butter is heating, dry cutlets with paper towels—do this just before putting them in pan. Then sauté cutlets 1 minute on each side. Using slotted metal spatula, transfer them directly to warm serving platter while completing sauce.

4. Add chicken stock to pan. Turn heat to high, scraping up any brown bits, and reduce stock by a little more than half. Add lemon juice and salt and pepper to taste, and cook another minute. Remove from heat and swirl in remaining 2 tablespoons butter until it is incorporated and sauce appears velvety.

5. Spoon sauce over chicken, coating it well. Garnish with lemon slices and parsley sprigs, if desired.

Braised Fresh Spinach and Mushrooms

1½ pounds spinach
1 medium-size onion
1 cup thinly sliced mushrooms (about ½ pound)
5 tablespoons butter
½ cup chicken stock
Salt
Freshly ground pepper
Freshly ground nutmeg

1. In large bowl, clean spinach thoroughly in several changes of cool water. Discard tough stems and any wilted leaves, and chop. Peel and chop onion. Wipe mushrooms clean with damp paper towels and slice thinly to make 1 cup.

2. In casserole, melt 3 tablespoons of the butter over medium-low heat. Add onion and sauté 4 to 5 minutes, until translucent but not browned. Add mushrooms and sauté another minute.

3. Turn heat to high, add stock, and bring to a boil.

4. Add spinach to casserole by handfuls, stirring constantly. Cover casserole and place in oven; bake 20 minutes.

5. Using slotted metal spoon, remove vegetables to heated serving dish. Put casserole on stove and over high heat reduce liquid to 2 tablespoons. Add remaining butter and a large pinch each of salt, pepper, and nutmeg. Pour over vegetables, toss well, and correct seasonings.

Cream of Lemon Soup
Fillets of Sole with Zucchini and Peppers
Blueberry Cream-Cheese Parfaits

Creamy lemon soup, garnished with sliced lemon and parsley, introduces the mustard-coated fillets of sole and the grated zucchini and red peppers. Follow this light meal with rich blueberry parfaits.

71

Only fresh lemon juice can give the creamy soup in this menu its sparkling clean flavor. Do not substitute bottled or frozen juice. A cautionary note: instead of pouring the beaten yolks directly into the hot chicken stock, which would scramble them, first add a little of the hot stock to the yolks, stirring constantly to avoid any lumpiness. Add a second ladleful of stock, continuing to stir. This heats the yolks through gently so they can be incorporated more easily with the stock.

Fillets of fresh sole or flounder, flattened to a quarter inch, bake quickly in a hot oven. You can cook the fillets in a baking pan or, as Peter Kump suggests, in stoneware or heatproof dinnerware. Before baking, spread mild, grainy mustard on both sides of the fillets. The grains, actually mustard seeds, add flavor and texture to the fillets without overpowering the delicate taste of the fish. When you shop, choose fish with firm, moist, odorless flesh. Store the fish well-wrapped in plastic or foil in the refrigerator and use it the same day.

The zucchini and red pepper mixture, sautéed quickly, is a colorful accompaniment to the fish and a nice contrast in texture.

The blueberry parfaits, which are part of the meal rather than an ADDED TOUCH, can be made with the other two dishes in under an hour. They taste like feathery-light cheesecake, and take only minutes to prepare. Peter Kump advises you to use only pure maple syrup rather than the blended or flavored syrups, because nothing matches the distinctive, delicate flavor of the pure syrup. When fresh blueberries are not in season, use frozen strawberries or raspberries in their own juice or orange sections soaked in orange-flavored liqueur. If you opt for the liqueur, eliminate the maple syrup.

WHAT TO DRINK

Muscadet, a bone-dry white, is a classic accompaniment to fish dishes like this one. A crisp Italian white wine, such as Verdicchio, is also compatible.

SHOPPING LIST AND STAPLES

1½ to 2 pounds fresh fillets of sole or flounder
1 pint blueberries
4 small zucchini
2 red bell peppers
2 lemons
2 shallots

Parsley sprigs (optional)
3 eggs
4 tablespoons unsalted butter
1 pint heavy cream
8-ounce package cream cheese
½ cup pure maple syrup plus 2 tablespoons (optional)
2 cups chicken stock, preferably homemade (see page 13), or canned
4 teaspoons coarse-grained French mustard, such as Moutarde de Meaux
1 teaspoon vanilla extract
⅓ cup confectioners' sugar
1 teaspoon vanilla extract
Whole nutmeg
Salt
Freshly ground pepper

UTENSILS

Food processor or grater
Medium-size sauté pan
1½-quart saucepan with cover
Ovenproof non-aluminum baking dish
Plate
Large mixing bowl
2 medium-size bowls
Colander
Strainer
Measuring cups and spoons
Chef's knife
Paring knife
2 wooden spoons
Metal spatula
Rubber spatula
Electric hand mixer
Nutmeg grater
Tongs
Soup ladle
Vegetable scrub brush

START-TO-FINISH STEPS

One hour ahead: Remove cream cheese from refrigerator.

1. Place medium-size bowl in refrigerator to chill. Follow fillets of sole recipe steps 1 and 2.
2. Follow blueberry parfait recipe steps 1 through 4.
3. Butter baking dish, chop shallots, and grate nutmeg.

Follow fillets of sole recipe steps 3 through 6.

4. Prepare lemon soup recipe steps 1 through 5 and serve.

5. Follow fillets of sole recipe steps 7 through 9 and serve.

6. For dessert, follow blueberry parfait recipe step 5.

RECIPES

Cream of Lemon Soup

2 lemons
2 cups chicken stock
1 cup heavy cream
3 egg yolks
Salt
Freshly ground pepper
4 sprigs parsley for garnish (optional)

1. Cut 4 thin slices from 1 lemon. Squeeze juice from leftover lemon and from second one into small bowl.

2. In 1½-quart saucepan, heat chicken stock until warm. Stir in cream. Turn off heat, cover, and keep warm.

3. In small bowl, lightly beat egg yolks with 2 tablespoons of the lemon juice. Pour in a ladleful of hot soup, stirring constantly. Repeat with another ladleful of soup.

4. Then, stirring constantly, pour yolk-lemon mixture into soup.

5. Taste for seasoning, adding additional lemon juice, salt, and pepper to heighten flavor, if desired. Ladle into soup bowls, float a lemon slice in each bowl, and garnish with parsley sprig, if desired.

Fillets of Sole with Zucchini and Peppers

4 small zucchini
1 teaspoon salt
2 red bell peppers
1½ to 2 pounds fresh fillets of sole or flounder
4 teaspoons coarse-grained French mustard, such as
    Moutarde de Meaux
3 tablespoons unsalted butter
2 shallots, peeled and chopped
Freshly grated nutmeg
Freshly ground pepper

1. Scrub zucchini well, cut off ends and discard; grate in food processor or with large holes of grater. Place grated zucchini in colander, toss with salt to mix evenly, and set over plate to drain at least 15 minutes.

2. Scorch red peppers by setting them directly over gas flame or under oven broiler, turning them with tongs until all sides are blistered and black. Place in a paper bag for 5 to 10 minutes.

3. With large, wet chef's knife, flatten fish fillets so that they are of even thickness, preferably about ¼ inch thick. Cut into serving pieces and, using rubber spatula, spread with mustard on both sides. Arrange in single layer in buttered ovenproof non-aluminum baking dish.

4. Preheat oven to 425 degrees.

5. Remove peppers from bag and peel them under running water. Slice open, remove seeds and ribs, and julienne. Set aside.

6. By handfuls, thoroughly squeeze all liquid from zucchini.

7. Bake fillets 4 to 6 minutes.

8. While fish is baking, melt butter over medium heat in medium-size sauté pan. Add shallots and sauté about 1 minute, or until translucent. Add zucchini and sauté another 2 minutes. Season to taste with freshly grated nutmeg and pepper. Add red pepper strips and continue to sauté 2 to 3 minutes.

9. With metal spatula, transfer fish fillets to dinner plates and serve with zucchini and red pepper mixture on the side.

Blueberry Cream-Cheese Parfaits

1 pint blueberries
½ cup pure maple syrup
4 ounces fresh cream cheese, at room temperature
⅓ cup confectioners' sugar
1 teaspoon vanilla extract
1 cup heavy cream, well chilled
Maple syrup for garnish (optional)

1. Pick over blueberries, carefully removing stems and any bruised or overripe fruit. Rinse well in strainer, drain, and transfer to medium-size bowl, reserving ¼ cup berries for garnish. Add maple syrup to bowl and stir to combine.

2. Using hand mixer, blend cream cheese with sugar and vanilla in large mixing bowl.

3. In chilled medium-size bowl whip cream until soft peaks form. Carefully fold cream into cream-cheese mixture just until combined. Fold in blueberries with syrup.

4. Divide mixture among 4 parfait glasses and refrigerate.

5. When ready to serve, garnish with reserved blueberries and drizzle on a little maple syrup, if desired.

Richard Sax

MENU 1 (Left)
Hearty Vegetable Chowder
Herbed Buttermilk Biscuits
Tossed Green Salad

MENU 2
Leek and Mushroom Tart
Mixed Vegetable Slaw

MENU 3
Individual Pumpkin Soufflés
Oven-Roasted Chicken Breasts
Rice Pilaf with Fresh Vegetables

L ike other zealous cooks, Richard Sax believes that beautiful food adds pleasure to life. Trained professionally in French and American kitchens where chefs spend money lavishly to prepare rich, complex recipes, he manages to streamline elegant concoctions into foods that even untrained home cooks can produce economically and quickly. He calls this "bringing food down to earth," yet his cooking is neither skimpy nor slapdash.

Because he is not a dogmatic cook, he likes to shift the emphasis of a meal, turning an appetizer or first course into a substantial entrée, especially when such a recipe features vegetables. He does this with the vegetable chowder of Menu 1 and with the leek and mushroom tart of Menu 2.

Another facet of his style—particularly in his soups, stews, and composed dishes—is his use of chunky ingredients to highlight their flavors and bright colors. He also likes strong, intense flavors such as mustard, vinegar, and hot peppers; a subtle version of this approach is his use of the nearly forgotten practice of seasoning pumpkin with pepper in his light pumpkin soufflés.

In this array of fresh vegetables—(clockwise from lower left) carrots, green beans, leeks, red peppers, onions, potatoes, corn, tomatoes, and peas—are some of the ingredients for the main-course chowder. Served with a tossed green salad and hot buttermilk biscuits, this is a substantial meal, suitable for any time of the year.

Hearty Vegetable Chowder
Herbed Buttermilk Biscuits
Tossed Green Salad

This hearty vegetable chowder uses vegetables that are available year round, but Richard Sax's vegetable choices are not mandatory. Instead of broccoli and beans, you may wish to use asparagus in season or snow peas; instead of corn, chick peas. There are numerous vegetables to cut up for the chowder, but, since it is the main course, you have little else to prepare. Vegetarians can omit the bacon and substitute vegetable stock for the chicken stock.

Most cooks would use a flour-fat roux to thicken this vegetable version of a traditional New England chowder recipe. Instead, Richard Sax thickens his chowder with some puréed onions, carrots, celery, and potatoes. Not only does this vegetable thickener produce a lighter soup, but it also intensifies the vegetable flavors.

WHAT TO DRINK

Try a light red wine, such as a Beaujolais or a California Gamay, to complement the robust chowder.

SHOPPING LIST AND STAPLES

½ pound bacon, thickly sliced
Small bunch broccoli
4 to 5 medium-size potatoes (about 1½ pounds)
¼ pound green beans
¼ pound mushrooms
2 red peppers
1 zucchini (optional)
½ pound fresh peas or 10-ounce package frozen (optional)
1 ear corn-on-the cob or 10-ounce package frozen corn
3 carrots
2 stalks celery
3 medium-size onions
3 radishes (optional)
1 head soft leaf lettuce, such as Boston or Bibb
Small head Romaine lettuce
1 bunch fresh herbs (parsley, chives, tarragon, or mixture)
1 clove garlic
1 stick plus 2 tablespoons butter (approximately)
1 cup milk
½ cup buttermilk
½ pint heavy cream
3 cups chicken stock, preferably homemade (see page 13), or canned

16-ounce can whole tomatoes
3 tablespoons olive oil
1½ tablespoons red wine vinegar
1 teaspoon Dijon mustard
2 cups flour
2 teaspoons baking powder
½ teaspoon baking soda
½ teaspoon sugar
Paprika
Mixed dried herbs (thyme, rosemary, and marjoram)
Salt and freshly ground black pepper

UTENSILS

Food processor or blender
Stockpot with cover
Small saucepan
Large baking sheet
Plate
Large salad bowl
Large mixing bowl
Small bowl
Colander
Strainer
Measuring cups and spoons
Chef's knife
Paring knife
Slotted spoon
Wooden spoon
Rubber spatula
Small whisk
Vegetable peeler
Pastry brush
Pastry blender (optional)
2- or 2½-inch biscuit cutter or round drinking glass
Salad spinner (optional)
Sifter (if not using food processor)

START-TO-FINISH STEPS

1. Cut bacon into ½-inch pieces and follow chowder recipe step 1.
2. Prepare vegetables for chowder: peel and dice onions; peel and slice carrots; slice celery; peel and dice potatoes; rinse broccoli, trim stem, and break into small flowerets; cut green beans; core, seed, and dice red peppers; scrub zucchini, if using, and slice; clean mushrooms with damp paper towel and slice. If using fresh corn, trim base, stand

corn on base end, and with sharp paring knife vertically slice kernels off cob. If using fresh peas, shell enough to make ½ cup. Drain canned tomatoes in strainer and chop.

3. Follow chowder recipe step 2.
4. For salad, slice radishes and mince garlic, if using. Chop herbs for biscuits.
5. Follow chowder recipe step 3.
6. Follow salad recipe step 1.
7. Follow chowder recipe step 4.
8. Follow herbed biscuit recipe steps 1 through 4.
9. Follow chowder recipe step 5.
10. Make dressing for salad, step 2.
11. Follow chowder recipe step 6, salad recipe step 3, and serve with hot biscuits.

RECIPES

Hearty Vegetable Chowder

½ pound bacon, thickly sliced, cut in ½-inch pieces
3 medium-size onions, peeled and diced
3 carrots, peeled and sliced
2 stalks celery, sliced
4 to 5 medium-size potatoes (about 1½ pounds), peeled and diced
3 cups chicken stock
Salt
Pinch of dried thyme
1 to 1½ cups small broccoli flowerets
¾ cup green beans, cut in 1½-inch lengths
2 red peppers, cored, seeded, and diced
1 zucchini, sliced (optional)
½ cup corn kernels
½ cup peas, preferably fresh, or frozen (optional)
¾ cup canned whole tomatoes, drained and chopped
1 cup sliced mushrooms
⅔ cup heavy cream
½ to 1 cup milk
Freshly ground black pepper
2 tablespoons butter (approximately)
Paprika

1. In stockpot, brown bacon over medium-low heat until golden but not crisp. With slotted spoon, transfer to paper-towel-lined plate; drain.
2. Add onions, carrots, and celery to bacon fat and sauté until onions are wilted, about 8 minutes.
3. Add potatoes, stock, salt to taste, and thyme, and stir to combine. Bring to a simmer and cook until potatoes are tender, about 15 minutes. Using slotted spoon, transfer about half of the vegetables to food processor or blender; reserve.
4. Add broccoli, green beans, red peppers, and zucchini, if using, to pot. Simmer, uncovered, until broccoli is just tender. Meanwhile, purée reserved vegetable in food processor or blender until smooth.
5. Return purée to soup; add corn, peas, if using, tomatoes, mushrooms, cream, ½ cup of milk, and bacon, and stir to combine. Simmer, uncovered, 5 minutes. If you like thinner chowder, add milk to desired consistency.

6. Taste soup and correct seasoning with salt and pepper if necessary. Top each serving with pat of butter and a sprinkling of paprika.

Herbed Buttermilk Biscuits

2 tablespoons butter (approximately)
2 cups flour
2 teaspoons baking powder
¾ teaspoon salt
½ teaspoon baking soda
½ teaspoon sugar
6 tablespoons cold butter
¼ cup chopped fresh herbs (parsley, chives, tarragon, or mixture)
½ cup buttermilk (approximately)

1. Preheat oven to 450 degrees. In small saucepan, melt butter and set aside. Lightly butter baking sheet. Sift together flour, baking powder, salt, baking soda, and sugar into mixing bowl. With 2 table knives or pastry blender, cut in cold butter until mixture is crumbly.
2. Add fresh herbs and about ⅓ cup of buttermilk. Using fork, stir mixture very gently, until it is soft but not sticky. Add more buttermilk as needed.
3. Gently turn out dough onto lightly floured surface, scraping sides of bowl with rubber spatula to loosen any clinging bits of dough. Pat to about ½-inch thickness. Using biscuit cutter, cut into 2- to 2½-inch rounds, and place on baking sheet. You should have about 12 biscuits.
4. Brush biscuits with melted butter and bake 12 to 14 minutes, until puffed and lightly golden. Serve hot, with additional butter.

Tossed Green Salad

1 head soft leaf lettuce, such as Boston or Bibb
Small head Romaine lettuce
3 radishes, thinly sliced (optional)
1½ tablespoons red wine vinegar (approximately)
Pinch dried herbs, including thyme, rosemary, and marjoram, or ½ teaspoon fresh herbs, including parsley
1 teaspoon Dijon mustard
1 clove garlic, minced (optional)
¼ teaspoon salt
½ teaspoon freshly ground pepper
3 tablespoons olive oil

1. Core lettuce and discard any bruised or discolored outer leaves. Wash lettuce under cold running water and dry in salad spinner or pat dry with paper towels. Tear into bite-sized pieces and place in salad bowl. Add radishes, if using. Cover and refrigerate until ready to serve.
2. In small bowl, whisk or stir together vinegar, herbs, mustard, garlic, salt, and pepper until smooth. In a slow, steady stream, add olive oil, whisking vigorously to combine. Correct seasoning, if necessary. Set dressing aside.
3. Just before serving, whisk or stir dressing to recombine and pour over salad; toss.

Leek and Mushroom Tart
Mixed Vegetable Slaw

Serve each guest a wedge of leek and mushroom tart, with a portion of the colorful vegetable slaw on the side.

The French *flamiche* and the Italian *porrata*, which are leek tarts, were the models for Richard Sax's savory and substantial leek and mushroom tart. Leeks, unknown in many American kitchens, are staples in Europe. Prized for their subtle, delicate flavor and versatility, they have a gentle onion taste that enhances rather than overpowers other ingredients.

WHAT TO DRINK

To complement the leek tart try a Chablis or a white Burgundy.

SHOPPING LIST AND STAPLES

6 thin slices ham (about 3 ounces)
8 slender leeks (about 1¾ pounds)
½ to ¾ pound mushrooms
½ cup snow peas (optional)
2 red bell peppers
2 carrots
1 large cucumber
4 radishes
Small bunch fresh parsley
2 eggs

1 stick plus 3 tablespoons unsalted butter
½ pint heavy cream
½ cup milk
¼ pound Swiss cheese
2 tablespoons vegetable oil
¼ cup vinegar, preferably rice wine vinegar
1½ cups flour
1 cup dried beans or rice
1 teaspoon sugar
Freshly grated nutmeg
Cayenne pepper
Salt and freshly ground pepper

UTENSILS

Food processor or grater
Large skillet with cover
9-inch tart or pie pan
3 large mixing bowls
Medium-size bowl
Small bowl
Measuring cups and spoons
Chef's knife
Paring knife
2 wooden spoons
Whisk
Nutmeg grater
Vegetable peeler
Rolling pin
Cooling rack

START-TO-FINISH STEPS

1. Follow tart shell recipe step 1.
2. Clean leeks and trim off tops and roots. Split lengthwise in half and rinse well under running water. Cut crosswise into slices. Clean and quarter mushrooms.
3. Complete tart shell recipe, steps 2 through 4.
4. Follow leek tart recipe steps 1 and 2. Sliver ham and, using food processor or grater, grate Swiss cheese. Chop parsley. Separate eggs and grate nutmeg.
5. Continue leek tart recipe, steps 3 through 5.
6. Prepare slaw vegetables; follow recipe steps 1 and 2.
7. When tart has rested, serve with slaw.

RECIPES

Leek and Mushroom Tart

8 slender leeks (about 1¾ pounds), trimmed, washed, halved lengthwise, and cut into 1-inch slices
3 tablespoons butter
Salt
1½ cups quartered mushrooms
1 cup slivered ham (about 6 slices)
½ cup freshly grated Swiss cheese
3 tablespoons chopped parsley
½ cup milk
½ cup heavy cream (or use more milk)

2 egg yolks
Pinch each of Cayenne pepper and grated nutmeg
Freshly ground pepper
1 partly baked 9-inch tart shell (see following recipe)

1. Preheat oven to 400 degrees.
2. Place leeks, 1 tablespoon of butter, 1 tablespoon cold water, and a little salt in large skillet. Cook over medium heat, covered, until leeks are slightly limp, about 10 minutes. Uncover and toss until liquid has evaporated, 1 to 2 minutes. Transfer to large mixing bowl.
3. Heat remaining butter in skillet and sauté mushrooms. Add mushrooms, ham, cheese, and parsley to mixture in bowl; toss to combine.
4. In medium-size bowl, whisk together milk, cream, egg yolks, Cayenne, nutmeg, and salt and pepper to taste.
5. Spread leek mixture in tart shell; place in oven and pour custard mixture over leeks. Bake 8 minutes, then lower heat to 375 degrees. Bake until set and lightly golden, 25 to 30 minutes. Let sit 5 minutes; cut into wedges.

Tart Shell

1½ cups flour
1 teaspoon salt
8 tablespoons cold butter
2 tablespoons cold water (approximately)
1 cup dried beans or rice (for weighting down pastry shell)

1. In large bowl, mix flour and salt, and cut in butter with 2 knives until mixture is crumbly. Stir in enough cold water so that pastry can be gathered into a ball. Wrap in wax paper and chill briefly.
2. Preheat oven to 400 degrees.
3. Roll out pastry, fit into 9-inch tart pan, and trim. Line with aluminum foil and fill with dried beans or rice. Bake shell until sides are set, 6 to 8 minutes.
4. Carefully remove foil and beans, and return shell to oven for about 8 minutes, until very pale gold. Remove from oven and set on cooling rack.

Mixed Vegetable Slaw

2 red bell peppers, seeded, cored, and cut into long, thin strips
1 large cucumber, peeled, halved lengthwise, seeded, and cut into long, thin strips
2 carrots, peeled, trimmed, and cut into long strips
4 radishes, thinly sliced
½ cup snow peas, cut lengthwise into strips (optional)
¼ cup vinegar
2 tablespoons vegetable oil
1 teaspoon sugar
½ teaspoon salt
Freshly ground pepper

1. Combine prepared vegetables in large mixing bowl.
2. In small bowl, stir together vinegar, oil, sugar, salt, and pepper. Correct seasonings to taste; use plenty of pepper. Pour dressing over vegetables and toss. Chill.

Individual Pumpkin Soufflés
Oven-Roasted Chicken Breasts
Rice Pilaf with Fresh Vegetables

Pumpkin soufflé is a light complement to this autumn meal of browned chicken breasts and vegetable-studded pilaf.

The pumpkin soufflés here are made without a flour-butter base, so they are exceptionally fragile. These do not rise as high as other soufflés, nor do they stay puffed once out of the oven.

If you use canned pumpkin purée, make sure it is the unsweetened variety, not the pie filling. To prepare fresh purée, split a pumpkin in half crosswise and scrape out the seeds and stringy material. Place halves cut-side down on a foil-lined baking sheet. Cover with foil and bake at 350 degrees, until tender, about 1½ hours. Cool, then scrape the flesh from the pumpkin shells and purée through a sieve or in a food processor.

WHAT TO DRINK

With this menu, the cook suggests a sprightly fruity white wine, such as an Italian Pinot Grigio or Tocai.

SHOPPING LIST AND STAPLES

2 large whole boneless chicken breasts with skin

2-pound fresh pumpkin, or 16-ounce can pumpkin

¼ pound green beans

¼ pound mushrooms

1 carrot

2 medium-size onions
2 scallions
Small bunch parsley
1 clove garlic
5 eggs
5 tablespoons unsalted butter
1¾ cups chicken stock, preferably homemade (see page 13), or canned
3 tablespoons maple syrup
2 tablespoons olive oil
1¼ cups long-grain rice
Flour or ground nuts
Freshly grated nutmeg
Cinnamon
Allspice
Salt and freshly ground pepper
2 tablespoons dry white wine

UTENSILS

Food processor (if using fresh pumpkin)
Large ovenproof skillet
Small skillet
Medium-size heavy-gauge saucepan with cover
Small baking pan
4 individual soufflé dishes or custard cups
2 large mixing bowls, 1 copper (if using whisk for soufflés)
Measuring cups and spoons
Chef's knife
Paring knife
Wooden spoon
Rubber spatula
Nutmeg grater
Electric hand mixer or whisk
Metal tongs

START-TO-FINISH STEPS

1. For soufflé recipe, peel and finely chop onion, separate eggs, grate nutmeg, and follow recipe steps 1 through 4.
2. Prepare vegetables for pilaf and follow recipe steps 1 through 4.
3. Follow soufflé recipe steps 5 and 6.
4. With flat side of chef's knife, crush garlic lightly and peel. Follow chicken recipe steps 1 through 3.
5. Follow pilaf recipe step 5, chicken recipe step 4, and serve with soufflés.

RECIPES

Individual Pumpkin Soufflés

1 tablespoon butter
Flour or ground nuts
3 tablespoons finely chopped onion
1½ cups pumpkin purée, fresh or canned
3 egg yolks
3 tablespoons maple syrup
½ teaspoon salt

¼ teaspoon freshly grated nutmeg
Pinch each of cinnamon, allspice, and freshly ground pepper
5 egg whites

1. Preheat oven to 425 degrees.
2. Butter 4 individual soufflé dishes or custard cups. Dust bottom and sides with flour or nuts; shake out excess.
3. In small skillet, heat 1 tablespoon butter over medium-low heat and sauté onion briefly, just until wilted.
4. In large mixing bowl, blend sautéed onion, pumpkin purée, egg yolks, maple syrup, salt, and spices.
5. In another large bowl, beat egg whites until stiff but not dry. Gently fold about one fourth of the whites into the pumpkin mixture; fold in remaining whites. Gently pour into dishes and smooth tops with spatula.
6. Bake until soufflés have puffed, 18 to 20 minutes.

Oven-Roasted Chicken Breasts

2 large whole boneless chicken breasts with skin (about 1 to 1¼ pounds each), halved
Salt and freshly ground pepper
1 clove garlic, lightly crushed and peeled
1 tablespoon butter
2 tablespoons olive oil

1. Trim off all fat and excess skin from chicken. Sprinkle lightly with salt and pepper. Rub with garlic.
2. Heat butter, oil, and garlic clove in ovenproof skillet large enough to hold chicken in single layer. When butter stops foaming, add breasts, skin side down. Sauté chicken over medium heat until skin is golden, about 5 minutes.
3. Place skillet in oven (after soufflés have cooked about 10 minutes). Open and shut oven door gently. Roast 5 minutes. Using tongs, turn breasts and roast 5 minutes.
4. Remove to dinner plates.

Rice Pilaf with Fresh Vegetables

2 tablespoons butter
1 tablespoon finely chopped onion
2 scallions, green and white portions, sliced
1 carrot, peeled and sliced
½ cup green beans, cut into 1- to 1½-inch lengths
½ cup sliced mushrooms
1¼ cups long-grain white rice
2 tablespoons dry white wine
1¾ cups chicken stock
2 tablespoons chopped parsley
Salt and freshly ground pepper

1. In medium-size heavy-gauge saucepan, heat butter over medium-low heat. Cook onion briefly until wilted.
2. Add vegetables and sauté about 3 minutes.
3. Add rice and toss to coat with butter. Cook, stirring, about 2 minutes. Add wine and boil briefly.
4. Add stock, stirring, and bring to a boil. Lower heat and simmer, partly covered, about 17 minutes, or until rice is tender. Remove from heat, cover, and keep warm.
5. Add parsley and salt and pepper to taste; fluff with fork.

Jean Grasso Fitzpatrick

MENU 1 (Right)
California Gazpacho
Artichoke Frittata
Roasted Peppers

MENU 2
Broiled Mushroom Caps
Risotto with Zucchini
Avocado and Red Pepper Salad

MENU 3
Penne with Broccoli Rabe
Stuffed Eggplant with Tomato Sauce
Fennel and Olive Salad

F ood writer Jean Grasso Fitzpatrick is a vegetarian who deals daily with the challenge of
preparing meals that both she and her strictly
vegetarian husband enjoy. This means, she says,
"being open to creative menu planning, beginning with all
the foods you both already enjoy: pasta, salad, cheeses,
pizzas, and most Chinese, Indian, and Middle Eastern
dishes." She strives to compose nutritionally complete
menus with courses that are compatible yet varied and
that are richly textured and flavorful.

Because she is interested in Italian culture, she often
borrows culinary techniques and ideas from Italy. For
instance, the main course of Menu 1 is a frittata, an Italian
open-faced omelet. It differs from the French version in
several ways: The frittata filling is stirred right into the
beaten eggs before they cook. The bottom is cooked slowly
over a low flame; then the top is browned quickly under the
broiler. Another distinctive Italian specialty, a braised
rice dish, or risotto, similar to pilaf, is the main course of
Menu 2. Menu 3 features an Italian-style entrée and a
pasta dish. Throughout the meal, Jean Grasso Fitzpatrick
uses several authentic Italian ingredients such as *broccoli
di rabe* (broccoli rabe) and fennel.

*A chunky gazpacho garnished with croutons begins this infor-
mal summer meal. Arrange a wedge of artichoke frittata and
strips of red and green peppers on each dinner plate and for
garnishing use a parsley sprig and slices of lemon and lime.
A basket of sliced French bread is an ideal accompaniment.*

82

California Gazpacho
Artichoke Frittata
Roasted Peppers

Gazpacho, a Spanish soup often nicknamed "liquid salad," is a refreshing summertime recipe that tastes best when vegetables are at their peak. The standard gazpacho recipe calls for puréed onions, tomatoes, green peppers, garlic, and cucumbers in varying proportions. For this version, Jean Grasso Fitzpatrick chops the vegetables rather than purées them, giving the soup a crunchy texture. Garnish each soup bowl with a heaping tablespoonful of croutons. You can make these by trimming the crusts off six slices of French or Italian bread, then cubing the slices. If you like garlic, mash 2 cloves on a cutting board by pounding the cloves with the flat side of a knife blade. Then rub both pulp and juice in a skillet. Discard the garlic, then add 3 tablespoons of olive oil to the skillet. Heat the oil and fry the bread cubes until they turn golden. Remove and drain the cubes on paper towels.

Like a French omelet, the Italian frittata is the base for an endless number of savory fillings. For this recipe, the cook uses fresh artichoke bottoms, mushrooms, and seasonings. Do not buy artichokes with leaves that open out, nor those that are turning brown—a sure sign of age or frost damage. Be sure you buy small artichokes, which cook through quickly. To prepare them for boiling, snap off the coarse inedible stems and pull off the tough outer leaves around the base of the artichoke head. With a sharp knife, slice off the top third of the leaves, then pare a thin layer from the tough bottom. Proceed with the recipe. If you prefer, you can use frozen artichoke hearts.

The roast-pepper recipe is a good example of how Italian cooks prepare vegetables simply, with an eye to heightening their natural flavors. To char the peppers, put them in the broiler or on the flame of a gas-stove burner. Once the outer skins blacken and blister, you peel them and are left with the sweet pepper flesh.

WHAT TO DRINK

It is difficult to match a wine with artichokes, but the eggs in this recipe help modify their strong flavor. The best choice here would be an uncomplicated dry white wine: the cook suggests an Italian Trebbiano.

SHOPPING LIST AND STAPLES

5 small artichokes or 9-ounce package frozen
   artichoke hearts

2 pounds ripe tomatoes
9 medium-size mixed red and green bell peppers
½ pound mushrooms
1 medium-size cucumber
Small head lettuce (optional)
1 lemon
1 small and 1 medium-size onion
1 clove garlic
6 eggs
2 tablespoons unsalted butter
¼ pound Parmesan cheese
6-ounce can tomato juice
¼ cup plus 4 tablespoons olive oil
2 tablespoons red wine vinegar
Hot pepper sauce
4 slices French or Italian bread
Whole nutmeg
Salt and freshly ground pepper

UTENSILS

Food processor or blender
Stockpot with cover
Medium-size ovenproof skillet
Small saucepan (if using frozen artichoke hearts)
15½-by-12-inch cookie sheet
Large bowl
Medium-size bowl
Colander
Measuring cups and spoons
Chef's knife
Paring knife
Wooden spatula
Metal tongs
Whisk
Cheese grater (if not using processor)
Nutmeg grater
Vegetable peeler

START-TO-FINISH STEPS

1. Follow frittata recipe step 1. Juice ½ lemon and grate Parmesan and nutmeg.
2. To make croutons: Preheat oven to 350 degrees. Cut bread slices into small cubes; trim off crusts. Bake on cookie sheet 3 to 4 minutes, or until lightly golden. Set aside.

3. Prepare vegetables for gazpacho and follow recipe steps 1 through 4. Chill bowls for gazpacho.
4. Prepare onion and mushrooms for frittata and follow steps 2 through 7.
5. Prepare roasted peppers, steps 1 through 4.
6. Follow frittata recipe step 8, gazpacho recipe step 5, and serve with the roasted peppers.

RECIPES

California Gazpacho

1 clove garlic, peeled and halved
1 small onion, peeled and cut into chunks
1 cucumber, peeled, seeded, and cut into 1-inch lengths
1 red bell pepper, cored, seeded, and cut into small pieces
2 pounds ripe tomatoes, cored, seeded, and coarsely chopped
1½ cups tomato juice, chilled
¼ cup olive oil
2 tablespoons red wine vinegar
Dash of hot pepper sauce
Salt
Freshly ground pepper
¾ cup croutons

1. Mince garlic and onion in food processor fitted with metal blade or in blender.
2. Add cucumber and red pepper, and chop briefly, pulsing machine on and off about 15 seconds. Do not mince.
3. Add remaining ingredients, except croutons; process just to mix. The soup should be coarsely textured.
4. Taste for seasonings and chill until serving time.
5. Serve in chilled bowls and garnish with croutons.

Artichoke Frittata

5 artichokes or 9-ounce package frozen artichoke hearts
Juice of ½ lemon
6 eggs
1 cup freshly grated Parmesan cheese
Pinch of freshly ground nutmeg
Salt
Freshly ground pepper
1 tablespoon olive oil
2 tablespoons unsalted butter
1 medium-size onion, chopped
1 cup sliced mushrooms

1. If using fresh artichokes, bring 4 quarts of water to a boil in covered stockpot. Trim artichoke stems, remove tough bottom leaves, and snip about an inch off top of artichokes. Add lemon juice to water and cook artichokes 15 to 20 minutes.
2. Drain artichokes in colander. Remove leaves. Carefully scoop out all of fuzzy choke. Cut hearts into quarters, and halve each quarter, if desired.
3. If using frozen artichoke hearts, cook in small saucepan according to package directions. Cut into quarters or slice thinly.

4. In large bowl, whisk eggs until frothy. Stir in cheese, nutmeg, and salt and pepper to taste.
5. In ovenproof skillet, heat olive oil and butter. Sauté onion, stirring with wooden spatula, until onion is soft. Add mushrooms and turn heat to medium-high for about 1 minute, sautéing mushrooms until they are barely heated.
6. Lower heat and pour in egg mixture. Add artichoke pieces, arranging them evenly in pan. Cook over low heat, without stirring, about 20 minutes, or until frittata is "set," and nearly cooked through.
7. While frittata is cooking, preheat oven broiler.
8. Leave frittata under broiler for 10 to 30 seconds to finish cooking and lightly brown top. Invert frittata onto serving plate. Serve warm, or at room temperature, cut into wedges.

Roasted Peppers

6 to 8 mixed red and green bell peppers
Juice of ½ lemon
3 tablespoons olive oil
Salt
Lettuce for garnish (optional)

1. Place peppers under broiler, close to heat source, and cook, turning them with tongs, until they are blackened and blistered on all sides.
2. Hold peppers under cold water; peel off skins with sharp paring knife. Pat dry with paper towels.
3. Core peppers; remove ribs and seeds. Cut peppers into long strips.
4. Combine lemon juice, olive oil, and salt in medium-size bowl. Add peppers, toss, and let marinate. Just before serving, arrange on bed of lettuce, if desired.

LEFTOVER SUGGESTION

Leftover frittata makes a delicious lunch the following day. Take it out of the refrigerator by midmorning so that it can warm up; it tastes better at room temperature than it does cold.

ADDED TOUCH

Bruschetta is toasted Italian bread, made with olive oil and garlic. It is quick to prepare, a crunchy accompaniment to the frittata.

Bruschetta

8 slices fresh Italian bread
2 cloves garlic, peeled and lightly crushed
2 tablespoons good-quality olive oil (approximately)

1. Preheat oven to 400 degrees.
2. Arrange bread slices in single layer on cookie sheet and toast in oven 3 to 5 minutes, or until golden.
3. Remove bread, rub each slice with crushed garlic, and drizzle with olive oil. Serve at once.

Broiled Mushroom Caps
Risotto with Zucchini
Avocado and Red Pepper Salad

Broiled mushroom caps and a risotto with thinly sliced zucchini are an attractive presentation for a light company lunch. Dress the salad with a ladleful of the thick dressing and sprinkle it with parsley.

For this vegetarian meal, broiled mushroom caps are an elegant appetizer that you can enjoy year round. Choose mushrooms that have not been chemically treated. Make sure that they have smooth, unmottled skins and caps that fit tightly over the stems. Wipe the mushrooms clean with a damp paper towel. Do not soak them, however, because they will become soggy. Save the stems in the refrigerator for use in soups or omelets.

For a good risotto, always use short-grained Italian rice, such as the arborio variety, which is available in Italian groceries and specialty food shops. This short-grained rice takes longer to cook than other varieties, and the pearly grains, creamy when cooked, stick to each other yet retain their firmness. You must cook the rice in two steps. First, in a heavy skillet, sauté the grains in fat, with the seasonings and vegetables, until the grains turn chalky white. Then, add the hot broth, ½ cup at a time, stirring constantly. Add more broth as the rice dries out—remember, this does not cook like standard boiled rice, so do not flood it with too much liquid at once.

WHAT TO DRINK

This meal would taste best with a brightly acid and fruity white wine, either an Italian Pinot Grigio or a California Chardonnay.

SHOPPING LIST AND STAPLES

1 pound medium-size mushrooms
4 medium-size zucchini
2 large, ripe avocados
3 medium-size red peppers
1 bunch parsley
1 small onion
1 clove garlic
4 tablespoons unsalted butter
¼ pound Parmesan cheese
1 cup ricotta cheese
5 cups chicken or vegetable stock, preferably homemade (see page 13), or water
¼ cup plus 2 tablespoons olive oil
¼ cup red wine vinegar
1½ cups short-grain rice, preferably arborio
1 teaspoon dried thyme
Salt
Freshly ground pepper

UTENSILS

Food processor (optional)
Medium-size saucepan
Large sauté pan
Broiler pan
Salad bowl
Measuring cups and spoons
Chef's knife
Paring knife
Metal spatula
Wooden spoon
Soup ladle
Cheese grater (if not using processor)

START-TO-FINISH STEPS

1. Prepare avocados and red peppers for salad, and follow recipe steps 1 and 2.
2. Follow broiled mushrooms recipe steps 1 and 2.
3. Prepare garlic, zucchini, and onion for risotto. Grate Parmesan with cheese grater or in food processor fitted with grating disc. Chop parsley, if using, for risotto and for mushrooms and salad.
4. Follow risotto recipe steps 1 through 3.
5. About 5 minutes before risotto is done, complete broiled mushrooms recipe, steps 3 and 4.
6. As soon as risotto is done, serve with the mushrooms and salad.

RECIPES

Broiled Mushroom Caps

1 pound medium-size mushrooms
2 tablespoons unsalted butter
1 teaspoon dried thyme
Salt
Freshly ground pepper
1 tablespoon chopped parsley for garnish (optional)

1. Remove mushroom stems and reserve for another use, such as in vegetable stock (see page 13). Clean caps with damp paper towels. Arrange mushrooms, cap side up, in broiler pan.
2. Preheat broiler.
3. Cut butter into small pieces and dot mushroom caps. Sprinkle caps with thyme and season with salt and pepper to taste.

4. Broil 2 or 3 minutes, or until butter melts and caps are golden. Remove to individual dinner plates with metal spatula. Garnish with parsley, if desired.

Risotto with Zucchini

2 tablespoons unsalted butter
2 tablespoons olive oil
1 clove garlic, chopped
4 medium-size zucchini, thinly sliced
1 small onion, chopped
5 cups chicken or vegetable stock, or water
1½ cups short-grain rice, preferably arborio
1 cup freshly grated Parmesan cheese
¼ cup chopped parsley
Salt and freshly ground pepper

1. In large sauté pan, heat butter and oil over medium-high heat. Add garlic, zucchini, and onion, and sauté until zucchini is lightly browned.
2. Heat stock or water in saucepan over high heat.
3. Add rice to zucchini mixture and, with wooden spoon, stir over low heat until rice absorbs the butter and oil. Add hot stock, a ladleful at a time, stirring after each addition; wait until rice absorbs each cup of stock before adding more. (Rice should take a total of about 30 minutes to cook.) When rice is cooked—the mixture should be creamy, not dry—stir in ½ cup of grated Parmesan, parsley, and salt and pepper to taste. Serve immediately; pass the remaining cheese separately.

Avocado and Red Pepper Salad

¼ cup red wine vinegar
1 cup ricotta cheese
Dash of salt
Freshly ground pepper
¼ cup olive oil
2 large, ripe avocados, halved, peeled, and cut into thin slices
3 red peppers, cored, seeded, and cut into thin strips
1 tablespoon chopped parsley for garnish (optional)

1. Pour wine vinegar into salad bowl and stir in the ricotta, salt, and pepper to taste. Slowly drizzle in olive oil, stirring constantly to blend.
2. Place avocado slices and pepper strips in salad bowl, and toss gently to coat with dressing. Sprinkle with parsley, if desired. Refrigerate, covered, until ready to serve.

Penne with Broccoli Rabe
Stuffed Eggplant with Tomato Sauce
Fennel and Olive Salad

Present this casual supper—baked stuffed eggplant arranged on a parsley-garnished platter, penne tossed with broccoli rabe and seasoned with a scattering of red pepper flakes, and white rings of fennel with black olives—all at the same time.

This substantial meal calls for two unusual vegetables: broccoli rabe and fennel. Broccoli rabe, or *broccoli di rabe*, as it is called in Italy, is a slightly bitter Italian green. The thin, firm stems, leaves, and tiny flowerets are all edible. Uncooked, it looks like a cross between spinach and regular broccoli, and it is delicious blanched, steamed, or boiled. You can find this green in well-stocked supermarkets, greengrocers, and Italian groceries in the late summer and fall. You can use regular broccoli instead, trimming and blanching the stalks, then cooking the pasta in the same water.

Fennel, another Italian vegetable, is also known as *finocchio*, Florence fennel, or anise, depending on where you shop. It is a refreshing, crunchy vegetable available in fall or winter and has a delicate anise flavor. Select fennel that has firm bulbs and creamy-white stalks.

A simple homemade tomato sauce moistens the eggplant stuffing mixture. Fresh tomatoes taste best when vine-ripened in season, but you can use canned plum tomatoes at other times of the year. Capers, which add piquancy to the stuffing, are sold in jars, packed either in vinegar or in salt. If you buy the salt-packed capers, rinse them well before using.

Broccoli rabe

WHAT TO DRINK

To enhance the vivid flavors of these dishes, you need a light, fruity red wine. The best choices would be a simple Chianti or a top-quality Valpolicella.

SHOPPING LIST AND STAPLES

1 pound broccoli rabe
1 pound fennel
2 to 4 eggplants (about 1 pound total weight)
1 pound tomatoes, or 16-ounce can peeled Italian plum
   tomatoes
Small bunch fresh basil, or 2 teaspoons dried
3 cloves garlic
½ pound mozzarella cheese

¼ pound Parmesan cheese
¼ pound black olives, preferably Italian
3½-ounce jar capers
¾ cup olive oil
2 tablespoons wine vinegar or 1 tablespoon sherry
     vinegar
1 pound penne or ziti
½ cup unseasoned dry bread crumbs
Crushed red pepper flakes
Salt and freshly ground pepper

UTENSILS

Food processor (optional)
Stockpot or large kettle
Medium-size sauté pan
Medium-size non-aluminum saucepan
Small saucepan
Baking dish
Serving bowl
Large bowl
Small bowl
Colander
Measuring cups and spoons
Chef's knife
Paring knife
2 wooden spoons
Cheese grater (if not using processor)
Whisk

START-TO-FINISH STEPS

1. Follow penne recipe step 1.
2. Using food processor or cheese grater, grate Parmesan for both penne and eggplant recipes. Dice mozzarella.
3. Peel, seed, and chop tomatoes, chop fresh basil, if using, and butter baking dish. Follow eggplant recipe steps 1 through 6.
4. While eggplant is baking, peel and chop garlic for penne and mince garlic for salad. Follow penne recipe steps 2 through 4.
5. Follow fennel salad recipe steps 1 through 3.
6. Follow penne recipe step 5 and serve with the eggplant and fennel salad.

RECIPES

Penne with Broccoli Rabe

1 pound broccoli rabe
1 pound penne or ziti
2 to 3 tablespoons olive oil
2 cloves garlic, peeled and chopped
½ cup freshly grated Parmesan cheese
Crushed red pepper flakes

1. In stockpot or large kettle, bring water to a boil for pasta.
2. Trim bottom of broccoli rabe. Wash stalks thoroughly;

halve crosswise and set aside in colander.
3. Add pasta to the boiling water and stir. Wait 2 minutes after water returns to a boil, then add broccoli rabe. Cook about 10 minutes, or until pasta is *al dente*.
4. Meanwhile, heat olive oil in small saucepan over medium heat and sauté garlic until lightly colored.
5. When cooked, drain pasta and broccoli rabe in colander. Transfer to serving bowl and toss with garlic and oil, Parmesan, and crushed red pepper flakes to taste.

Stuffed Eggplant with Tomato Sauce

4 tablespoons olive oil
2 tablespoons chopped fresh basil, or 2 teaspoons dried
2 cups peeled, seeded, and chopped tomatoes, fresh or
     canned Italian plum
2 to 4 eggplants (about 1 pound)
2 tablespoons capers
½ pound mozzarella, diced (approximately 2 cups)
½ cup freshly grated Parmesan cheese
Salt
Freshly ground pepper
½ cup unseasoned dry bread crumbs

1. In medium-size non-aluminum saucepan, heat 2 tablespoons of the olive oil. Add basil and tomatoes, and cook over low heat 10 minutes.
2. Preheat oven to 425 degrees.
3. Split eggplants lengthwise. Being careful not to puncture the skins, hollow out with paring knife, leaving shells about ½ inch thick. Place shells in buttered baking dish.
4. Chop eggplant pulp into ½-inch dice. Heat remaining 2 tablespoons of olive oil in sauté pan and sauté pulp briefly, stirring, until softened, about 3 minutes. Remove from heat.
5. In large bowl, combine pulp with capers, mozzarella, Parmesan, and half of tomato sauce. Season with salt and pepper to taste. Fill eggplant shells with mixture, sprinkle with bread crumbs, and top with remaining tomato sauce.
6. Bake 15 to 20 minutes, until crust forms on top. Cool briefly before serving.

Fennel and Olive Salad

1 pound fennel
12 black olives, preferably Italian
¼ cup olive oil
2 tablespoons wine vinegar, or 1 tablespoon sherry
     vinegar
1 clove garlic, minced
Salt
Freshly ground pepper

1. Trim fennel stalks and remove leafy tops. Rinse and pat dry with paper towels. Slice fennel thinly and place in serving bowl.
2. Pit olives and add to fennel.
3. In small bowl, whisk remaining ingredients together. Pour over fennel and olives, and toss to coat.

Barbara Tropp

MENU 1 (Left)
Savory Tofu Stew
Stir-Fried Rice with Bell Peppers and Almonds

MENU 2
Pot-Browned "Noodle Pillow"
Stir-Fried Curried Pork with Onions
Hot-and-Sour Hunan-Style Vegetables

MENU 3
Wine "Explosion" Mushroom Soup
with Sweet Peas
"Old Egg" with Scallions and Shrimp
Stir-Fried Velvet Spinach with Glass Noodles

Most Westerners assume that Chinese cuisine accentuates meats and fish, but, according to Barbara Tropp, China scholar turned cook: "In the Chinese world, vegetables have preeminence. The Chinese love to keep the character of the vegetable intact." They never serve raw vegetables. Instead, the Chinese cook them until just crisp-tender to bring out their full, natural flavor, as she does with the red peppers in the stir-fried recipe of Menu 1.

Traditionally, the Chinese prize freshness, which is why Barbara Tropp does not include canned vegetables in her recipes. If a vegetable is unavailable fresh, she advises you to select another. You must think of your recipe as a mixture of contrasting tastes and textures, then include a vegetable you enjoy. One dish in Menu 3 is stir-fried spinach and glass noodles. If perfectly fresh, crisp spinach is not available, try kale or an Oriental spinach-like green such as *bok choy*.

When Chinese cooks prepare produce for a multi-vegetable recipe, they slice each differently. For the Hunan-style vegetables of Menu 2, for instance, the cook directs you to slice the zucchini and carrots in different widths, so that they cook evenly. For the entrée in that meal, she uses sliced pork loin or—in an alternate version—an exotic ingredient, gluten, as a centerpiece for the vegetables. Also known as "mock meat," this high-protein product is made from wheat gluten and formulated to have a meaty texture.

Fresh ginger, almonds, tofu, mushrooms, red pepper, egg, green pepper, scallions, and carrots are ubiquitous Chinese ingredients. They are combined in this menu to produce a savory tofu stew, shown here in a Chinese sand pot, as well as a colorful stir-fried rice dish with green and red peppers and whole almonds.

Savory Tofu Stew
Stir-Fried Rice with Bell Peppers and Almonds

The combination of the tofu stew and stir-fried rice provides enough color, texture, and complementary proteins to comprise a complete dinner without any meat. Tofu is a soybean product that is low in fat. Often used in Oriental cooking, it is available in supermarkets.

You can find black soy sauce in Chinese markets or specialty food shops. You will also need either a Chinese black vinegar or balsamic vinegar for the stew. Black vinegar is usually available in Chinese markets.

WHAT TO DRINK

Chinese flavors are best accompanied by good German wine—a Riesling, for instance. But the cook, a red wine lover, also recommends a robust Italian or French red: a Côtes du Rhône or a Barbera.

SHOPPING LIST AND STAPLES

6 squares white Chinese-style tofu (about 1½ pounds)
1 pound slender carrots
⅓ pound medium-size or large white mushrooms
2 large bell peppers, preferably red
1 bunch medium-size scallions
4 large cloves garlic
2-inch length fresh ginger
3 large eggs
1¾ cups unsalted chicken or vegetable stock, preferably
    homemade (see page 13), or canned
5 to 6 cups plus 5 to 6 tablespoons corn or peanut oil
3 tablespoons black soy sauce
1½ to 2 tablespoons Chinese black vinegar or balsamic
    vinegar
1 cup rice
8 medium-size or 6 large dried Chinese black mushrooms,
    preferably the flower variety
2½-ounce package blanched whole almonds
1 tablespoon light brown sugar
Kosher salt and freshly ground black pepper
Freshly ground white pepper
2 teaspoons Chinese rice wine or dry sherry

UTENSILS

14-inch wok
    or Dutch oven with cover (for frying tofu)
    and large cast-iron skillet (for stir frying rice)
12-inch Chinese sand pot
    or 12-inch heavy casserole with cover
Medium-size saucepan with tight-fitting lid
2 baking sheets
Large dinner plate
Large bowl
6 small bowls
2 large strainers
Measuring cups and spoons
Thin-bladed Chinese cleaver or chef's knife
Paring knife
Metal wok spatula or metal spatula
Slotted metal spoon or Chinese mesh spoon
16-inch chopsticks or wooden spoon
Wooden tongs (optional)
Vegetable peeler
Deep-fat thermometer
Scissors

START-TO-FINISH STEPS

The night before or in the morning: Prepare rice for stir-fried rice recipe, steps 1 through 6.

1. Preheat oven to 300 degrees.
2. Trim and cut scallions into 1-inch lengths, slice ginger into 4 quarter-size rounds, and follow tofu stew recipe steps 1 through 15.
3. Wipe out wok, if using. In small bowl, beat eggs with fork and set aside until ready to use. Follow rice recipe steps 7 through 16. Heat serving bowl for rice in oven.
4. Follow tofu stew recipe step 16, stir-fried rice recipe step 17, and serve.

RECIPES

Savory Tofu Stew

8 medium-size or 6 large dried Chinese black mushrooms
6 squares white Chinese-style tofu (about 1½ pounds)
5 to 6 cups corn or peanut oil
1 pound slender carrots
⅓ pound medium-size or large fresh white mushrooms
4 medium-size whole scallions, cut into 1-inch lengths
4 quarter-size slices fresh ginger
4 large cloves garlic
1¾ cups unsalted chicken or vegetable stock
3 tablespoons black soy sauce
1 tablespoon light brown sugar, firmly packed

1½ tablespoons Chinese black vinegar or balsamic vinegar
Kosher salt and freshly ground black pepper

1. In small bowl, soak dried mushrooms in hot water to cover until fully soft and spongy, 20 to 30 minutes.
2. Cut tofu into large triangles by cutting across both diagonals of each square to yield 24 triangles.
3. Place tofu, cut sides down, on baking sheet lined with a triple layer of paper towels.
4. Set wok or Dutch oven over high heat. Add oil to a level 1¼ inches below rim and heat.
5. Peel carrots. Cut on diagonal at 1-inch intervals, rolling carrot a third of a turn away from you after each cut.
6. Clean fresh mushrooms and trim any woody stems. Halve or quarter mushrooms, including stems.
7. Smack scallions and ginger lightly with broad side of cleaver. Smack each clove of garlic similarly and discard peel. In small bowl, combine scallions, ginger, and garlic. In another small bowl, combine stock, soy sauce, brown sugar, and vinegar.
8. Line another baking sheet with a double layer of paper towels and set beside baking sheet with tofu.
9. When oil registers 375 degrees on deep-fat thermometer, hot enough so that a bit of tofu bobs to surface within 2 seconds, carefully add tofu triangles to oil one by one. Shield yourself from any spattering; do *not* cover pot. With chopsticks or wooden spoon, poke triangles gently to separate them. Adjust heat to maintain temperature: there will be a crown of white bubbles around each triangle. If necessary, fry tofu in 2 batches, being certain to let oil reheat to 375 degrees before frying second batch.
10. Fry tofu triangles until evenly golden brown, about 4 minutes, turning them with chopsticks or wooden tongs. With slotted metal spoon or Chinese mesh spoon, remove them to drain on prepared paper-towel-lined baking sheet.
11. Turn off heat and carefully move pot to a back burner. (When it has cooled, you can strain oil and store for reuse.)
12. Drain black mushrooms, snip off stems with scissors, and rinse caps briefly under cool water to dislodge any sand trapped in gills. If caps are very large, cut them in half with scissors.
13. Stir stock mixture, then pour into sand pot or heavy casserole. If you are using a sand pot, bring liquids to a simmer over low heat. Otherwise, simmer over high heat.
14. Add black mushrooms and scallion mixture to pot. Cover and simmer 5 minutes.
15. Add tofu, carrots, and fresh mushrooms. Stir gently to baste them with sauce, cover, and simmer until carrots are tender, 20 to 30 minutes. Lift lid after 10 minutes to check simmer and gently stir stew to redistribute ingredients.
16. Turn off heat and stir stew. Taste and adjust seasonings, adding a dash more vinegar or sugar to obtain a rich flavor. Add Kosher salt and pepper to taste.

Stir-Fried Rice with Bell Peppers and Almonds

1 cup rice
½ cup blanched whole almonds
2 large bell peppers, preferably red
5 to 6 tablespoons corn or peanut oil
3 large eggs, beaten
2 teaspoons Chinese rice wine or dry sherry
1 teaspoon Kosher salt
Freshly ground white pepper

1. Place rice in large bowl with cold water to cover. With your hand, stir in circles 15 to 20 seconds. Drain in strainer. Dry bowl.
2. Transfer rice to saucepan. Add 1½ cups water for short- or medium-grain rice, 1¾ cups for long-grain rice, and bring to a rolling boil over medium-high heat.
3. When starchy bubbles climb nearly to rim, in about 30 seconds, cover and reduce heat to maintain a slow, bubbly simmer. Do not lift lid until removing rice from pan.
4. Simmer rice 15 minutes. Remove from heat and let rest 20 minutes.
5. Remove cover and gently fluff rice with fork to separate grains. Spread rice in thin layer on baking sheet to cool.
6. When thoroughly cool, transfer to the large bowl used for soaking, cover, and refrigerate until needed.
7. Spread almonds on baking sheet and toast in oven until golden, about 5 minutes, shaking sheet occasionally. Transfer to small bowl and set aside. Turn off oven.
8. Cut peppers in half lengthwise; core, seed, and remove white ribs. Cut lengthwise into ½-inch strips. Holding strips together, cut them crosswise into ½-inch squares.
9. Using your fingers, toss the cold rice. Have all ingredients plus dinner plate within easy reach.
10. Heat wok or skillet over high heat until hot enough to evaporate a bead of water on contact. Coat bottom and lower sides of pan with 2½ tablespoons of oil, then reduce heat to medium-high. When oil is hot enough to puff 1 drop of egg on contact, beat eggs again and add to pan. They should puff and bubble around the edge immediately. Pause until film of cooked egg sets on bottom. With spatula, push cooked egg to far side of pan, so liquid egg will flow into center. Continue until just set, then scrape onto plate and break into small bits.
11. Wipe pan with wet paper towel, leaving thin film of oil, and return it to high heat.
12. When pan is hot enough to evaporate a bead of water on contact, add 2 tablespoons oil, swirl to coat bottom, and reduce heat to medium-high. When hot enough to sizzle a pepper square, add peppers and, using spatula, toss to glaze and heat through, 15 to 20 seconds, adjusting heat so peppers sizzle without scorching.
13. Add wine to pan, pause several seconds, then stir briskly to glaze peppers with wine essence.
14. Add rice and toss to combine. Heat about 1 to 2 minutes; lower heat if rice begins to scorch. If necessary, drizzle in more oil from side of pan to prevent sticking.
15. When rice is hot, add salt and toss to combine. Taste for seasoning; add salt and pepper to taste.
16. Add eggs, tossing gently to combine, and heat through, about 10 seconds. Turn off heat; keep covered.
17. Just before serving, add almonds and stir to combine. Turn rice into heated serving bowl.

Pot-Browned "Noodle Pillow"
Stir-Fried Curried Pork with Onions
Hot-and-Sour Hunan-Style Vegetables

Barbara Tropp's name for the pan-fried noodles in this menu is "noodle pillow." Quickly cook the noodles and drain them. Form a pillow by coiling noodle strands in a hot skillet. Brown pillow on each side, as you would a pancake. If possible, use fresh, Chinese egg noodles, which come in one-pound bags. You can refrigerate extra noodles for up to a week or freeze them for several months. If you cannot find the Chinese variety, substitute fresh or dried Italian vermicelli. You can prepare this recipe a day

Serve the curried pork on a bed of crisp pan-fried noodles, which have been pre-cut for easier handling. The hot-and-sour vegetables, displayed in a shallow dish, offer a variety of taste, color, and texture.

or two ahead: just boil, drain, and toss the noodles with oil and salt; then store them in a covered container in the refrigerator.

Both Northern and Southern Chinese use curry in a limited number of stews, favoring a flavor that is fruitier than that of the more familiar, sharp-and-spicy Indian curries. The pork recipe here calls for curry paste, an oil-based mixture of spices, turmeric, and hot chilies. Available in Chinese groceries, it will keep indefinitely in your pantry. If you use the gluten alternate, pay careful attention to the recipe directions for this version. Some of the steps and techniques are different, and you will not need the curry paste. The "Companion" brand of canned, curry-braised gluten is the one Barbara Tropp recommends. You

can buy it at many large Chinese markets. In either case, you will need regular soy sauce and black sesame seeds. A regular, or thin and light, soy sauce is mild tasting and ideal for adding both color and taste to cooking liquids. Black sesame seeds are a standard Chinese garnish, desirable for their flavor and texture. Toasting them first, which is optional, intensifies the nutty flavor. They are available in Chinese markets and should be stored in airtight jars in your refrigerator.

For the vegetable recipe, you need two other typically Oriental ingredients: salted black soybeans and rice vinegar. The black beans are a popular seasoning agent used in many kinds of sauces. They come in plastic bags, bottles, or jars and, once opened, last indefinitely in an airtight container on your pantry shelf. Avoid brands that contain Chinese five-spice powder; these are too potent for most recipes. A white rice vinegar, whether Chinese or Japanese, has a clean, refreshing taste that is fuller than that of a Western white vinegar. Rice vinegars are sold in the gourmet section of many supermarkets.

WHAT TO DRINK

The cook favors a hearty red wine for this menu, either a Petite Syrah or a Zinfandel. Ice-cold beer or ale are tradi-tional beverages served with highly seasoned Chinese dishes; either one would be a good accompaniment to the lively spices featured here.

SHOPPING LIST AND STAPLES

¾-pound well-trimmed boneless pork loin, or 10-ounce can Curry-Braised Gluten (Curry Chai Chi Jou), preferably Companion brand
¾-pound Chinese cabbage (with broad, tightly wrapped, light green leaves)
1 head cauliflower (to yield ¾ pound flowerets)
1 pound firm, slender zucchini
½ pound carrots
2 large yellow onions
3 cloves garlic
1-inch length fresh ginger
1 cup plus 1½ tablespoons unsalted chicken or vegetable stock, preferably homemade (see page 13), or canned
1 cup plus 6 tablespoons corn or peanut oil
¼ cup plus 2½ tablespoons light soy sauce
2 tablespoons unseasoned Chinese or Japanese rice vinegar
2 teaspoons Oriental sesame oil

3 to 4 teaspoons curry paste

¾ pound thin, fresh or frozen Chinese egg noodles, or Italian vermicelli

2 tablespoons Chinese salted black beans (not the variety seasoned with five-spice powder)

2 tablespoons black sesame seeds

2 tablespoons cornstarch

¾ teaspoon dried red pepper flakes

2 teaspoons sugar

Kosher salt

UTENSILS

Stockpot or kettle with cover

2 woks or 2 twelve-inch heavy-gauge skillets with covers, preferably cast iron

Heatproof serving bowl

Large plate (optional)

2 large bowls

Medium-size bowl

2 small bowls plus additional bowl (if using alternate recipe)

Large colander

Strainer (if using alternate recipe)

Measuring cups and spoons

Thin-bladed Chinese cleaver or chef's knife

Paring knife

Metal spatula or metal wok spatula

Wooden spoon

16-inch chopsticks or wooden spoon

Vegetable peeler

START-TO-FINISH STEPS

1. If using frozen noodles, thaw and follow noodle pillow recipe step 1.

2. While water comes to a boil, follow stir-fried curried pork recipe steps 1 through 4.

3. Follow noodle pillow recipe steps 2 through 6.

4. Follow Hunan-style vegetables recipe steps 1 through 5.

5. Preheat oven to 250 degrees. Heat serving platters or bowl for vegetables and for noodle pillow.

6. Follow noodle pillow recipe steps 7 and 8.

7. In small bowl or cup, dissolve cornstarch in stock or water. Cook hot-and-sour vegetables, steps 6 through 12, and keep warm in oven.

8. Cook other side of noodle pillow, steps 9 through 11.

9. Follow curried pork recipe steps 5 through 8.

10. Remove vegetables and noodle pillow from oven. Follow noodle pillow recipe step 12, curried pork recipe step 9, and serve at once with vegetables.

RECIPES

Pot-Browned "Noodle Pillow"

¾ pound thin Chinese egg noodles, fresh, or frozen and thoroughly defrosted, or Italian vermicelli

2 teaspoons Oriental sesame oil

1½ teaspoons Kosher salt

5 to 7 tablespoons corn or peanut oil

1. In covered stockpot or kettle, bring 3 to 4 quarts of warm, unsalted water to a boil over high heat.

2. In large colander, gently fluff noodles with your fingers to separate strands.

3. Add noodles to pot and cook 3 to 4 minutes until still firm but just cooked through, swishing occasionally with chopsticks or handle of wooden spoon.

4. Drain immediately in colander, then refresh under cold running water until chilled, turning noodles with your hands, once they have begun to cool, to chill them evenly. Shake colander several times to remove excess water from noodles.

5. Spread noodles on large, lint-free towel, then roll it up into loose tube and gently pat to dry noodles, just as you would dry a sweater.

6. Remove noodles to large bowl, sprinkle with sesame oil and salt, then gently toss strands with your fingers, glazing and separating them. Be careful not to break noodles as you toss them.

7. Heat skillet or wok over high heat until hot enough to evaporate a bead of water on contact. Add 4 or 5 tablespoons vegetable oil, depending on size of pan, then swirl to glaze sides and bottom of pan. Reduce heat to medium.

8. When oil is hot enough to sizzle a single noodle, add noodles, coiling them evenly in pan and working from outer perimeter to the center. Press down with spatula, cover pan, and cook until bottom is evenly golden brown, 5 to 7 minutes. Check after a minute and adjust heat if required so that noodles sizzle gently in oil and begin to steam.

9. With spatula, loosen browned noodles, then flip pillow over with sharp jerk of your wrist, or slide pillow onto inverted pot lid or large plate; invert holder and slip noodles back into pan, browned side up.

10. Drizzle remaining oil in from side of pan, then shake gently to distribute oil underneath noodles. Press pillow down with spatula, cover pan, and cook until browned, 5 to 7 minutes more.

11. With spatula, loosen noodles, if needed, then slip them onto round, heated serving platter. If necessary, you can hold noodle pillow in preheated 250-degree oven.

12. For easy serving, cut noodle pillow into wedges with knife, before topping with stir-fried curried pork or gluten. It will not appear cut and will be very easy to serve.

Stir-Fried Curried Pork with Onions

¾-pound well-trimmed boneless pork loin, or 10-ounce can Curry-Braised Gluten (Curry Chai Chi Jou)

1 tablespoon cornstarch

1½ or 1¾ teaspoons sugar

4 tablespoons light soy sauce

2 large yellow onions

¾ pound Chinese cabbage (with tightly wrapped, light green leaves)

3 to 4 teaspoons curry paste
½ cup unsalted chicken or vegetable stock
7 to 9 tablespoons corn or peanut oil
Kosher salt
2 tablespoons black sesame seeds

1. For pork recipe, using cleaver or chef's knife, cut meat against grain into even slices a scant ⅛-inch thick and 2 inches wide. In large bowl, combine cornstarch, 1½ teaspoons sugar, and 3 tablespoons soy sauce, stirring well to blend. Add pork, then toss well with your fingers to coat each slice.

For alternate recipe: Omit cornstarch mixture. Drain the gluten in strainer set over small bowl; reserve liquid. Cut gluten into ⅛-inch strips.

2. Using either Chinese cleaver or chef's knife, halve onions lengthwise, peel, then cut crosswise into arcs ¼-inch thick.

3. Leaving cabbage intact for quick cutting, slice crosswise into strips ½ inch wide. Cut base piece(s) where strips do not separate into pie-type wedges, then combine wedges and strips in medium-size bowl.

4. For pork recipe, in small bowl, combine curry paste, stock, ¼ teaspoon sugar, and 1 tablespoon soy sauce, stirring to blend. For alternate recipe, omit this entire step and all these ingredients.

5. Heat wok or skillet (that is deep enough to accommodate onions and cabbage) over high heat until hot enough to evaporate a bead of water on contact. Add 4 tablespoons oil, swirl to glaze pan, then reduce heat to medium-high. When hot enough to sizzle a piece of onion, add onions and toss gently to glaze and separate pieces, adjusting heat to maintain a sizzle without scorching onion; drizzle in a bit more oil from side of pan if onions become too dry. Continue to toss until onions soften, 3 to 4 minutes.

6. Add cabbage and toss briskly to combine with onions. Sprinkle with salt and continue to toss until cabbage is lightly glazed and hot, about 1 minute, adjusting heat to maintain a sizzle and drizzling in a bit more oil from side of pan if needed.

7. For pork recipe, transfer vegetables to medium-size bowl, cover, and keep warm. Wipe pan clean and return it to high heat until hot enough to evaporate a bead of water on contact. Add 3 tablespoons oil, swirl to coat bottom of pan, then reduce heat to medium-high. Add pork and toss briskly to separate slices. When pork is 90 percent gray, add curry mixture and vegetables, and toss 1 minute to combine thoroughly.

For alternate recipe: Leave vegetables in pan, add gluten strips, and toss to combine. Add reserved gluten liquid, stirring to blend. Raise heat to bring liquids to a simmer. Cover pan and simmer 2 to 3 minutes, until onions and cabbage have absorbed the liquid's color and flavor and liquid is reduced by about two thirds.

8. Turn off heat, stir, and sprinkle with 1 tablespoon of sesame seeds. Stir to combine. Taste and adjust seasoning, if necessary.

9. Mound on pot-browned noodle pillow and sprinkle with remaining sesame seeds.

Hot-and-Sour Hunan-Style Vegetables

1 head cauliflower (to yield ¾ pound flowerets)
½ pound carrots
1 pound firm, slender zucchini
1 tablespoon finely minced ginger
1 tablespoon finely minced garlic
2 tablespoons Chinese salted black beans (not seasoned with five-spice powder)
¾ teaspoon dried red pepper flakes
½ cup unsalted chicken or vegetable stock
2½ tablespoons light soy sauce
2 tablespoons unseasoned Chinese or Japanese rice vinegar
¼ teaspoon sugar
4 to 6 tablespoons corn or peanut oil
1 tablespoon cornstarch dissolved in 1½ tablespoons cold stock or water

1. Tear off leaves from base of cauliflower. Using paring knife, cut flowerets from cauliflower. Cut any large flowerets into walnut-size pieces.

2. Trim and peel carrots. Using Chinese cleaver or chef's knife, cut carrots on diagonal into thin coins, ⅛ inch thick.

3. Trim tips from zucchini, then cut crosswise into rounds ¼ inch thick. (The quickest way to do this is to line several zucchini up side by side, then cut them crosswise at once using cleaver or long chef's knife.)

4. Combine ginger, garlic, salted black beans, and pepper flakes in small bowl. With wooden spoon, combine stock, soy sauce, vinegar, and sugar in another small bowl, and leave spoon in bowl.

5. Have all ingredients within easy reach of your stovetop.

6. Heat wok or skillet over high heat until hot. Add 4 tablespoons oil, swirl to glaze pan, then reduce heat to medium-high. When oil is hot enough to sizzle a bit of ginger mixture, add it to pan. With wooden spoon, stir gently until fragrant, about 15 seconds, adjusting heat so mixture foams without scorching.

7. Add cauliflower and toss briskly about 1 minute, to glaze flowerets evenly and start them cooking. Lower heat if they begin to scorch, and drizzle in a bit more oil from side of pan if cauliflower becomes dry.

8. Add carrots and toss about 1 minute more, until evenly glazed, hot, and edges curl slightly; adjust heat and add more oil if needed.

9. Add zucchini and toss about 30 seconds, drizzling in a bit more oil if slices look dry.

10. With wooden spoon, stir sauce ingredients and add them to pan. Toss well to combine, then raise heat to bring liquids to a simmer. Adjust heat to maintain a steady simmer, cover pan, and simmer 1 minute. Stir, test for doneness, then cover and simmer another 30 to 60 seconds, if zucchini is not quite tender-crisp.

11. Reduce heat to low when zucchini is done. Stir cornstarch mixture to recombine, add it to pan, then toss until mixture turns glossy, about 15 seconds.

12. Remove vegetables to heatproof serving bowl and keep warm in oven until ready to serve.

Wine "Explosion" Mushroom Soup with Sweet Peas
"Old Egg" with Scallion and Shrimp
Stir-Fried Velvet Spinach with Glass Noodles

Wine "explosion" soup with mushrooms and peas precedes the light entrée—a Chinese-style soufflé and spinach with noodles.

In this light meal, suitable for a mild spring evening, the soup functions as a fragrant beverage for the soufflé and the vegetables. Serve all three dishes at once, just as a Chinese family would do.

The Chinese delight in whimsical names for their recipes. Here, wine "explosion" describes the sizzle in the classic Chinese technique of adding wine to hot oil. This evaporates the alcohol and traps the wine essence as the base for the soup. Barbara Tropp uses a mixture of dried and fresh mushrooms to give the broth its dusky character. Dried black mushrooms, highly valued in Chinese cooking, have a fragrant, smoky taste and, after soaking, a velvety texture. The soaking also makes them spongy enough to cut into pieces. Dried mushrooms are available from Chinese groceries or specialty food shops; they keep indefinitely on your pantry shelf.

A variety of fresh mushrooms is now available at several types of outlets. Western button mushrooms can be bought all year in most supermarkets—look for perfect, white or cream-colored caps. Mild Japanese enokitake, which look like miniature umbrellas, shiitake (the Japanese term for the Chinese dried black mushroom in its fresh form), and pearly oyster mushrooms can be found in Oriental markets and in some Western markets. Golden, trumpet-shaped chanterelles grow wild, but, unless you are a trained mycologist, you should look for them at quality greengrocers.

"Old egg," another Chinese whimsy, describes the Chinese version of soufflé, cooked for a long time (hence, old) on top of the stove. Unlike the French soufflé, this version puffs best when you chill the eggs before you beat them. Beat them only slightly; beat whites and yolks together. This recipe takes only a few minutes to assemble and about a half hour to cook.

Glass noodles, more commonly called bean threads, are sold in cellophane packets in Chinese markets or in the gourmet food section of some supermarkets. Made from mung-bean starch, they turn transparent when cooked.

Bean threads require soaking in either hot or boiling water, depending on where they were manufactured. Bean threads from Taiwan or Thailand need hot water; boiling water makes them gelatinous. Those from the People's Republic of China need boiling water. Regardless of the brand, soak bean threads still wrapped in their rubber-band or string binding; otherwise they become too unmanageable to cut.

Oriental sesame oil, used for seasoning rather than cooking, has the rich nutty aroma of toasted sesame seeds. For this recipe, do not buy the Middle Eastern, cold-pressed sesame varieties, which have a very different flavor.

If you wish to prepare this meal partly beforehand, you can make the soup, blanch the spinach, and soak the bean threads and the dried mushrooms a day in advance.

WHAT TO DRINK

The cook's preference here is for a light red wine with character, such as a Beaujolais. If you prefer tea with Chinese dishes, try a slightly acidic imported variety like Water Goddess or Dragon Well.

SHOPPING LIST AND STAPLES

½ cup tiny bay shrimp or ¼ pound small shrimp
2 pounds spinach, preferably with stems and rosy root ends intact
½ pound fresh mushrooms (choose 1 or 2 types: white button, enokitake, shiitake, oyster, or chanterelles)
½ pound unshelled peas, or 10-ounce package frozen peas
1 bunch scallions
4 shallots (optional)
8 large eggs
4⅓ cups unsalted chicken or vegetable stock, preferably homemade (see page 13), or canned
½ cup plus 1 tablespoon corn or peanut oil
2 teaspoons Oriental sesame oil
1½ teaspoons light soy sauce
2 ounces bean threads (glass noodles)
8 large dried Chinese black mushrooms, preferably thick-capped flower variety
2 teaspoons sugar
Kosher salt
Freshly ground pepper
2 tablespoons Chinese rice wine or dry sherry (approximately)

UTENSILS

2½- or 3-quart heavy Dutch oven, casserole, or small stockpot with tight-fitting cover
Wok or large, heavy-gauge skillet
Large saucepan with cover
Medium-size non-aluminum saucepan with cover
Small saucepan with cover
Large bowl
Medium-size bowl
2 small bowls
Colander
Strainer
Measuring cups and spoons
Thin-bladed Chinese cleaver or chef's knife
Paring knife
Chinese metal wok spatula or metal spatula
Wooden spoon
Whisk (optional)
Scissors

START-TO-FINISH STEPS

1. If using fresh peas for soup, shell enough to measure ½ cup; if using frozen peas, set them out to thaw. Mince shallots or scallions to measure 2 tablespoons. Follow mushroom soup recipe step 1.
2. Follow stir-fried spinach recipe step 1.
3. Follow old egg recipe step 1. Slice scallion rings to measure 4 tablespoons.
4. Heat 3 to 4 cups of water in teakettle to required temperature for soaking bean threads. Follow stir-fried spinach recipe steps 2 through 8.
5. Follow old egg recipe steps 2 through 6.
6. Follow mushroom soup recipe steps 2 through 9.
7. Follow stir-fried spinach recipe steps 9 and 10, old egg recipe step 7, and serve with the soup.

RECIPES

Wine "Explosion" Mushroom Soup with Sweet Peas

8 large dried Chinese black mushrooms
½ pound fresh mushrooms (choose 1 or 2 types: white button, enokitake, shiitake, oyster, or chanterelles)
4 cups unsalted chicken or vegetable stock
½ cup green peas, fresh or frozen and defrosted
2 to 4 tablespoons corn or peanut oil
2 tablespoons finely minced shallots or thinly cut scallion rings, from green and white sections
1½ tablespoons Chinese rice wine or dry sherry
Pinch of sugar
Kosher salt

1. In small bowl, soak dried mushrooms in hot water to cover until fully soft and spongy, 20 to 30 minutes.
2. Drain mushrooms, snip off stems with scissors, and rinse caps briefly under cool water to dislodge any sand trapped in gills. Using Chinese cleaver or chef's knife, cut caps into large strips about ⅛ inch thick.
3. Prepare fresh mushrooms: Clean button mushrooms by bobbing them briefly in small bowl of cool water. With paring knife, remove any woody stem tips, then cut mushrooms into umbrella-shaped slices ⅟₁₆ inch thick. Enokitake, shiitake, and oyster mushrooms do not need to be washed. Separate enokitake into small clusters and remove any very spongy stem ends. Separate oyster mush-

rooms into small clusters. Using paring knife, remove any tough shiitake stems, then cut caps into ⅛-inch slivers. With damp paper towel, wipe chanterelles clean, then cut into thin arcs or strips, following natural trumpet-like curve of mushroom.

4. In small saucepan, combine dried mushrooms, stock, and fresh peas, if using. (Do not add frozen peas until later.) Cover, bring to a slow simmer over high heat, and adjust heat to maintain a steady simmer. Simmer, covered, 5 minutes.

5. Heat non-aluminum saucepan over high heat until hot enough to evaporate a bead of water on contact. Add 2 tablespoons oil, swirl to coat bottom, then heat until hot enough to sizzle a pinch of shallot. Add shallots or scallions and stir with wooden spoon until fully fragrant, 10 to 15 seconds, adjusting heat so they foam without browning. Splash in wine, pause a second or two for it to explode in a fragrant hiss, then add fresh mushrooms. Stir fry until soft, about 4 minutes, drizzling in more oil from side of pan only if mushrooms are sticking. There should be no excess liquid in pan.

6. When mushrooms are soft, add simmering stock mixture to the pan. Bring to a simmer, stirring with wooden spoon, then cover and simmer 5 minutes.

7. Reduce heat to low and taste soup. Add sugar to enrich wine flavor, then season carefully with salt to bring out flavor of mushrooms.

8. Add frozen peas, if using, and stir several times until heated through.

9. Turn off heat and keep covered until ready to serve. The soup keeps perfectly, growing richer as it sits. If required, reheat it over low heat before serving.

"Old Egg" with Scallion and Shrimp

½ cup tiny bay shrimp or cubed small fresh shrimp (about ¼ pound)
1 teaspoon Chinese rice wine or dry sherry
Several twists freshly ground pepper
8 chilled large eggs
4 tablespoons thinly cut scallion rings, from green and white sections
⅓ cup unsalted chicken or vegetable stock
1½ teaspoons light soy sauce
Kosher salt
2 tablespoons corn or peanut oil

1. If using small shrimp, shell, devein, and cube them with sharp paring knife. In small bowl, toss shrimp and wine. Sprinkle with pepper and toss again.

2. In large bowl, lightly beat eggs with whisk or fork. Add scallion rings, stock, and soy sauce. Taste and add salt if necessary. Add shrimp mixture and stir gently to blend.

3. Heat Dutch oven, casserole, or stockpot over high heat until hot enough to evaporate a bead of water on contact. Add oil, swirl to coat bottom and sides of pot, then use oil-soaked paper towel to wipe oil film around sides of pot up to lip.

4. When oil is hot enough to slowly bubble a drop of egg in

about 30 seconds, stir egg mixture gently, swirl pot to redistribute oil, then add egg mixture to pot.

5. Cover tightly and cook over low heat 25 minutes.

6. After 25 minutes, peek quickly under lid. If egg is not puffed to within 1½ inches of lip, *gently* replace cover and cook 5 to 10 minutes more.

7. Bring pot swiftly to the table, lid still on (the soufflé will usually sink once lid is lifted). Call for attention, lift lid to display soufflé, then cut into wedges for serving.

Stir-Fried Velvet Spinach with Glass Noodles

2 pounds spinach
2 ounces bean threads (glass noodles)
3 tablespoons corn or peanut oil
1¼ teaspoons Kosher salt
½ to 1 teaspoon sugar
2 teaspoons Oriental sesame oil

1. In large covered saucepan, bring 2 to 2½ quarts of unsalted water to a boil over high heat.

2. Discard any straggly spinach leaves and white roots, then use scissors to cut stems and large leaves into 2-inch sections. Cut bulky stem clusters into 2 or 3 pieces through base; leave small stem clusters and any red root tips intact. In large bowl, plunge cut spinach into several changes of cold water, gently pumping up and down to remove grit. Drain in colander and shake off excess water.

3. Plunge spinach into boiling water.

4. After 1 minute, drain spinach in colander, flush with cold running water until chilled, then press lightly with palms of hands to remove excess water. Fluff spinach gently to loosen mass.

5. In medium-size bowl, cover bean threads with 3 to 4 cups of heated water, without removing binding of rubber bands or strings. If bean threads are from Taiwan or Thailand, use hot water; if they are from the People's Republic of China, use boiling water.

6. When pliable, after about 10 seconds, use scissors to cut through loop ends or center of skein, thereby cutting bean threads into manageable 4- to 5-inch lengths. Cut rubber bands or strings and discard them, then swish bean threads to disperse in water.

7. After another 10 to 15 seconds, when bean threads are firm—like rubber bands to the touch—rinse briefly with cool water and drain again.

8. Have all ingredients within easy reach of your stovetop.

9. Heat wok or skillet over high heat until hot enough to evaporate a bead of water on contact. Add oil, swirl to coat pan, then reduce heat to medium-high. When hot enough to sizzle a bit of spinach on contact, add spinach and toss briskly to separate leaves and glaze them with oil, 15 to 20 seconds. Sprinkle with salt and sugar, then continue to toss briskly another minute. Add noodles and, using spatula, blend with several quick stirs until heated through. Add sesame oil, toss briskly to combine, then remove from heat.

10. Arrange several rosy-tipped spinach stems on top, if desired, and serve at once.

Acknowledgments

The Editors particularly wish to thank the following for their contributions to the conception and production of these books: Ezra Bowen, Judith Brennan, Angelica Canon, Elizabeth Schneider Colchie, Sally Dorst, Florence Fabricant, Marion Flynn, Lilyan Glusker, Frieda Henry, Jay Jacobs, Pearl Lau, Kim MacArthur, Kay Noble, Elizabeth Noll, Fran Shinagel, Martha Tippin, Ann Topper, Jack Ubaldi, Joan Whitman.

The Editors would also like to thank the following for their courtesy in lending items for photography: *Cover:* cloth—The Basket Handler; platter—Mayhew; quiche pan—Pottery Barn. *Pages 18–19:* aluminum pan—Farberware; red pan—Copco. *Page 22:* handpainted cloth—Peter Fasano; napkin—Katja; basket—F. O. Merz; plates—Metlox; flatware—Conrans. *Page 24:* cloth—Brunschwig and Fils; napkin—Leacock and Company; basket—F. O. Merz; dish—Far Eastern Arts, Inc. *Pages 26–27:* mat—Sturbridge Village Catalogue; napkin—Leacock and Company; plate—George Briard; flatware—Wallace Silversmiths. *Page 30:* cloth, plates—Pottery Barn; flatware—The Lauffer Company. *Page 33:* handwoven cloth—Solveig Fernstrom-Umbach; basket—Pottery Barn; china—Buffalo China Inc. *Pages 36–37:* grids, baskets, plates, casseroles—Pottery Barn; server—Wallace Silversmiths. *Page 40:* stoneware—Pottery Barn. *Pages 42–43:* countertop—Formica® Brand Laminate by Formica Corp.; pitcher—Buffalo China Inc.; plates, dishes—Conrans. *Pages 46–47:* tiles—Laura Ashley; napkin—Katja; plate—Pottery Barn. *Page 50:* cloth, napkin—Conrans; mat, tray, plate, bowl—Pottery Barn; flatware—The Lauffer Company. *Page 52:* cloth—Brunschwig and Fils; bowls—Conrans. *Pages 54–55:* cloth, candle holders, platters—Museum of American Folk Art Shop; teapot—Janis Schneider from Downtown Potters' Hall; white plates—Laura Ashley; flatware—The Lauffer Company. *Page 58:* cloth—Leacock and Company; runner—Katja; napkin—Fabrications; white tray—Eigen Arts Pottery; platter—Conrans. *Page 61:* napkin—Leacock and Company; pan—Bazar Français. *Pages 64–65:* cloth, mats, napkins, platters, plates, glasses—Pierre Deux; flatware and servers, vase—The Lauffer Company. *Page 71:* cloth—Laura Ashley; napkin—Leacock and Company; plate—Laura Ashley; flatware—Wallace Silversmiths. *Pages 74–75:* pot—Farberware; bowls—Buffalo China Inc. *Page 78:* countertop—Formica® Brand Laminate by Formica Corp.; napkins, trays, plates, glasses—Pottery Barn; flatware—The Lauffer Company. *Page 80:* cloth—Leacock and Company; mat, napkin—D. Porthault, Inc.; plate—Baccarat. *Pages 82–83:* cloth—Brunschwig and Fils; napkin—Leacock and Company; pottery—Terrafirma; flatware—The Lauffer Company. *Page 86:* flatware—Wallace Silversmiths. *Page 88:* pottery—Terrafirma. *Pages 90–91:* grill—Pottery Barn; blue bowl—Dean & DeLuca. *Pages 94–95:* handpainted cloth—Peter Fasano; platter—Dean & DeLuca; bowl—Williams-Sonoma. *Page 98:* glass, dishes—Dean & DeLuca; flatware—Williams-Sonoma.

Photograph of Richard Sax, page 5: © Copyright Thomas Victor.

Illustrations by Ray Skibinski
Production by Giga Communications

Index

Acorn squash, 10
almonds
  and bell peppers with rice, stir-fried, 91–93
  popovers with Amaretto butter, 27, 33–35
  with wild rice, 55, 61–63
Amaretto butter, almond popovers with, 27, 33–35
apple and celeriac salad, 64, 69–70
artichokes
  frittata, 82–85
  selection and storage of, 9
Asian-style dishes
  saffron millet with stir-fried tofu and snow peas, 55–57
  see also Chinese-style dishes
asparagus, 9
avocados
  orange and lettuce salad, 30, 32
  and red pepper salad, 82, 86–87
  selection and storage of, 10

Baking, 13
balsamic vinegar, 15
basmati rice, 22
bean curd, *see* tofu
beans
  black-eyed peas and green beans with rice pilaf, 18, 20–21

lima, and dill with Persian-style rice, 18, 22–23
beets
  chocolate cake, spicy, 45
  with peas and tomatoes, 25
  salad, 64–67
bell peppers
  and almonds with rice, stir-fried, 91–93
  and avocado salad, 82, 86–87
  roasted, 82–85
  sauce, broiled scrod with, 47, 50–51
  selection and storage of, 10
  and zucchini with fillet of sole, 64, 71–73
Bibb lettuce
  and escarole with herbed vinaigrette, 36, 42–45
  and Romaine lettuce tossed salad, 75–77
biscuits, herbed buttermilk, 75–77
black-eyed peas and green beans with rice pilaf, 18, 20–21
blanching, 11
blueberry cream-cheese parfaits, 64, 71–73
boiling, 11
bok choy, 15
  selection and storage of, 9
Boston lettuce

and escarole with herbed vinaigrette, 36, 42–45
  with fennel and radicchio salad, 47, 52–53
  and Romaine tossed salad, 75–77
braising, 12
bread crumbs, 15
breads
  bruschetta, 85
  herbed buttermilk biscuits, 75–77
broiling, 13
bruschetta, 85
broccoli
  omelets, puffed, 55, 61–63
  selection and storage of, 9
broccoli rabe, 88 *illus.*
  with penne, 82, 88–89
  selection and storage of, 9
brown butter and caper sauce, turkey scallops with, 64–67
brown rice with mushrooms, 18, 24–25
bulb vegetables
  selection and storage of, 9
  see also onions
butter, 15
  Amaretto, almond popovers with, 27, 33–35
  and caper sauce, turkey scallops with, 64–67

clarified, 12
  sautéing with, 12
buttermilk biscuits, herbed, 75–77
butternut squash, 10

Cabbage
  selection and storage of, 9
  shredding, 11
cake, chocolate beet, 45
California gazpacho, 82–85
canned vegetables, 7, 9
capers, 14
  and brown butter sauce, turkey scallops with, 64–67
carotene-rich vegetables, 8
carrots
  and horseradish salad, 64–67
  marinated, 36, 40, 41
casserole, 17 *illus.*
cauliflower
  with garlic and sesame seeds, 18, 22–23
  selection and storage of, 9
celeriac and apple salad, 64, 69–70
celery, 9
chalupas, guacamole, 55, 58–60
Cheddar cheese, 15
cheese
  cream, and blueberry parfaits, 64, 71–73

fondue with chilies (chilies con queso), 55, 58–60
goat, fried, with Romaine lettuce, 27–29
and scallion enchiladas with guacamole sauce, 47–49
types of, 15
chicken breasts
oven roasted, 75, 80–81
in parchment with mushrooms and tomatoes, 27–29
piccata, 64, 69–70
with vegetables and sweet-and-sour sauce, 36, 42–45
chicken stock, 13
chilies con queso (chilies with cheese fondue), 55, 58–60
Chinese black mushrooms
stir-fried with tofu and snow peas, 56–57
wine "explosion" soup with sweet peas, 91, 98–100
Chinese black vinegar, 15
Chinese cabbage, 15
Chinese parsley, 15
Chinese-style dishes
hot-and-sour Hunan-style vegetables, 91, 94–97
"old egg" with scallions and shrimp, 91, 98–100
pot-browned "noodle pillow," 91, 94–96
savory tofu stew, 91–93
stir-fried curried pork with onions, 91, 94–97
stir-fried rice with bell peppers and almonds, 91–93
stir-fried velvet spinach with glass noodles, 91, 98–100
wine "explosion" mushroom soup with sweet peas, 91, 98–100
chives, 9
chocolate
beet cake, spicy, 45
glaze, 45
chopping, 11
chowder, vegetable, 75–77
cilantro, 15
cinnamon and oranges, 36–39
coarse salt, 14
colander, 16, 17 illus.
cooking techniques, 11–13
cooking tools, 16, 16–17 illus.
coriander, 15
Cox, Beverly, 4
menus of, 36–45
cream-cheese blueberry parfaits, 64, 71–73
cucumbers
hot-and-sour salad, 55–57
selection and storage of, 10
and tomato with yogurt, 18, 22–23
cumin seeds with peas and tomatoes, 18, 24–25
curried dishes
pork with onions, stir-fried, 91, 94–97

pumpkin purée, 55, 61–63
cutting vegetables, 10–11

Deep-dish vegetable pot pies, 27, 30–32
desserts
baked pears, 32
blueberry cream-cheese parfaits, 64, 71–73
pineapple ice, 35
spicy chocolate beet cake, 45
strawberries in liqueur with ice cream, 53
dicing, 11, 63 illus.
dill and lima beans with Persian-style rice, 18, 22–23

Eggplant
pie, 36–39
selection and storage of, 10
in spicy tomato sauce, 18, 20–21
stuffed, with tomato sauce, 82, 88–89
in yogurt, 21
eggs, 15
artichoke frittata, 82–85
individual pumpkin soufflés, 75, 80–81
"old egg" with scallions and shrimp, 91, 98–100
puffed broccoli omelets, 55, 61–63
electric appliances, 16
enchiladas, cheese and scallion, with guacamole sauce, 47–49
endive, 9
equipment, 8, 16, 16–17 illus.
escarole and lettuce with herbed vinaigrette, 36, 42–45

Fat for sautéing, 12
fennel
with Boston lettuce and radicchio salad, 47, 52–53
and olive salad, 82, 88–89
selection and storage of, 9
fennel seeds, 20
fish
broiled scrod with red-pepper sauce, 47, 50–51
fillets of sole with zucchini and peppers, 64, 71–73
Fitzpatrick, Jean Grasso, 5
menus of, 82–89
flour, 14
Freiman, Jane Salzfass, 4
menus of, 47–53
frittata, artichoke, 82–85
frozen vegetables, 7–8, 9
fruit, 15
baked pears, 32
tarts, 32
fruit-vegetables, 7
selection and storage of, 10
see also names of vegetables

Garden vegetable sauce, spaghetti squash with, 27, 33–35
garlic, 14
selection and storage of, 9

and sesame seeds with cauliflower, 18, 22–23
gazpacho, California, 82–85
ginger (fresh), 15
coarse chopping, 20
glass noodles with spinach, stir-fried, 91, 98–100
glaze, chocolate, 45
goat cheese, 15
fried, with green salad, 27–29
graters, 16 illus., 17 illus.
green beans
and black-eyed peas, with rice pilaf, 18, 20–21
and onion salad, 36–39
with sweet-and-sour sauce, 64–67
green onions, see scallions
green salad
with fried goat cheese, 27–29
with herbed vinaigrette, 36, 42–45
with oranges, 27, 30–32
tossed, 75–77
guacamole
chalupas, 55, 58–60
cheese and scallion enchiladas with, 47–49

Ham and shrimp stuffed Louisiana-style mirlitons, 36, 40–41
herbed buttermilk biscuits, 75–77
herbed vinaigrette, green salad with, 36, 42–45
herbs, 14
see also names of herbs
horseradish and carrot salad, 64–67
hot-and-sour dishes
cucumber salad, 55–57
Hunan-style vegetables, 91, 94–97
hubbard squash, 10
Hunan-style vegetables, hot-and-sour, 91, 94–97

Ice cream, strawberries in liqueur with, 53
immature flower vegetables
selection and storage of, 9
see also names of vegetables
Italian-style dishes
artichoke frittata, 82–85
Boston lettuce, fennel, and radicchio salad, 47, 52–53
fennel and olive salad, 82, 88–89
pasta with mushroom sauce, 47, 52–53
penne with broccoli rabe, 82, 88–89
risotto with zucchini, 82, 86–87
stuffed eggplant with tomato sauce, 82, 88–89

Jaffrey, Madhur, 4
menus of, 18–25
jalapeño peppers, 58
julienne vegetables, 11

Kale, 9
knives, 16, 17 illus.
Kosher salt, 14
Kump, Peter, 5
menus of, 64–73

Leafstalk vegetables
selection and storage of, 9
see also names of vegetables
leafy green vegetables
selection and storage of, 9
see also names of vegetables
leeks, 14, 44 illus.
and mushroom tart, 75, 78–79
storage of, 9
legumes, 9–10
lemon juice, 15
lemon soup, cream of, 64, 71–73
lettuce
and escarole with herbed vinaigrette, 36, 42–45
and fennel with radicchio salad, 47, 52–53
with fried goat cheese, 27–29
and orange salad, 27, 30–32
selection and storage of, 9
shredding, 11
tossed salad, 75–77
types of, 15
lima beans and dill with Persian-style rice, 18, 22–23
liquids, cooking with, 11–12
liquors for flavoring, 15
Louisiana-style mirlitons stuffed with ham and shrimp, 36, 40–41

Mexican-style dishes
cheese and scallion enchiladas with guacamole sauce, 47–49
chilies con queso (chilies with cheese fondue), 55, 58–60
guacamole chalupas, 55, 58–60
rice, 55, 58–60
seafood salad, 47–49
millet, saffron, 55–57
mincing, 11
mint with yogurt, 24–25
mirlitons stuffed with ham and shrimp, Louisiana-style, 36, 40–41
Monterey Jack cheese, 15
mozzarella cheese, 15
mushrooms, 7
with brown rice, 24–25
caps, broiled, 82, 86–87
and leek tart, 75, 78–79
sauce, pasta with, 47, 52–53
selection and storage of, 10
and spinach, braised, 64, 69–70
and tomatoes with chicken in parchment, 27–29
wine "explosion" soup with mushrooms and sweet peas, 91, 98–100
mustard greens, 9
mustards, 15

Napa, 15
new potatoes, steamed, 47, 50–51
noodles, 14
    pot-browned "pillow," 91, 94–96

Oils, 14
    cooking with, 12–13
    "old egg" with scallions and
        shrimp, 91, 98–100
    olive and fennel salad, 82, 88–89
    olive oil, 14
omelets, broccoli, puffed, 55,
    61–63
onions
    dicing, 63 illus.
    and green bean salad, 36–39
    scallions, see scallions
    selection and storage of, 9
    stir-fried and curried with
        pork, 91, 94–97
    and tomato salad, 64–67
    types of, 9, 14
oranges
    and cinnamon, 36–39
    and lettuce salad, 27, 30–32
oven cooking, 13

Pans, 12, 16, 17 illus.
pantry, 14–15
parboiling, 11
parfaits, blueberry cream-cheese,
    64, 71–73
Parmesan cheese, 15
parsley, 15
pasta, 14
    with mushroom sauce, 47,
        52–53
    penne with broccoli rabe, 82,
        88–89
    pot-browned "noodle pillow,"
        91, 94–96
pattypan squash, 10
pearl onions, 9
pears, baked, 32
peas
    selection of, 9
    snow peas stir-fried with tofu,
        55–57
    with tomatoes and beets, 25
    and tomatoes with cumin seeds,
        18, 24–25
    with wine "explosion" mush-
        room soup, 91, 98–100
penne with broccoli rabe, 82,
    88–89
pepper, 14
peppers
    see bell peppers
    chilies con queso (chilies with
        cheese fondue), 55, 58–60
Persian-style rice with lima beans
    and dill, 18, 22–23
pie
    eggplant, 36–39
    vegetable, 27, 30–32
pilaf
    with black-eyed peas and green
        beans, 18–21
    with vegetables, 75, 80–81

pineapple ice, 35
popovers, almond, with Amaretto
    butter, 27, 33–35
pork, stir-fried and curried with
    onions, 91, 94–97
potatoes, 7
    new, steamed, 47, 50–51
    selection and storage of, 9
    types of, 9
pot-browned "noodle pillow," 91,
    94–96
pot pies, vegetable, 27, 30–32
pots, 16, 17 illus.
poultry
    turkey scallops with brown but-
        ter and caper sauce, 64–67
    see also chicken
pumpkin
    purée, curried, 55, 61–63
    selection and storage of, 10
    soufflés, individual, 75, 80–81

Radicchio, Boston lettuce, and
    fennel salad, 47, 52–53
red peppers, see bell peppers
rhubarb, 9
rice, 15
    with bell peppers and almonds,
        stir-fried, 91–93
    brown, with mushrooms, 18,
        24–25
    Persian-style, with lima beans
        and dill, 18, 22–23
    pilaf with black-eyed peas and
        green beans, 18–21
    pilaf with vegetables, 75, 80–81
    risotto with zucchini, 82, 86–87
    Spanish, 55, 58–60
    wild, with almonds, 55, 61–63
ricotta cheese, 15
risotto with zucchini, 82, 86–87
roll cutting, 11
Romaine lettuce
    with fried goat cheese, 27–29
    and leaf lettuce tossed salad,
        75–77
root vegetables
    selection and storage of, 9
    see also names of vegetables
rutabagas, 9

Safflower oil, 14
saffron, 14
    millet, 55–57
salad
    avocado and red pepper, 82,
        86–87
    beet, 64–67
    Boston lettuce, fennel, and
        radicchio, 47, 52–53
    carrot and horseradish, 64–67
    celeriac and apple, 64, 69–70
    green bean and onion, 36–39
    guacamole chalupas, 55, 58–60
    herbed vinaigrette with let-
        tuce, 36, 42–45
    hot-and-sour cucumber, 55–57
    marinated carrots, 36, 40, 41
    mixed vegetable slaw, 75,
        78–79

olive and fennel, 82, 88–89
orange and lettuce, 27, 30–32
Romaine lettuce with fried goat
    cheese, 27–29
seafood, 47–49
spaghetti squash, 35
tomato and onion, 64–67
tossed green, 75–77
yogurt with tomato and
    cucumber, 23
salt, 14
sautéing, 12
sauté pan, 12, 17 illus.
Sax, Richard, 5
    menus of, 75–81
scallions, 14
    and cheese enchiladas with
        guacamole sauce, 47–49
    and shrimp with "old egg," 91,
        98–100
    storage of, 9
scrod, broiled, with red-pepper
    sauce, 47, 50–51
seafood
    salad, 47–49
    see also fish; shrimp
seed pod vegetables
    selection and storage of, 9–10
    see also names of vegetables
seed vegetables
    selection and storage of, 9–10
    see also names of vegetables
sesame oil, 14
sesame seeds and garlic with
    cauliflower, 18, 22–23
shallots, 14
    storage of, 9
sherry vinegar, 15
shredding, 11
shrimp
    and ham stuffed Louisiana-
        style mirlitons, 36, 40–41
    and scallions with "old egg," 91,
        98–100
Shulman, Martha Rose, 5
    menus of, 55–63
slaw, mixed vegetable, 75, 78–79
slicing, 11
snow peas, stir-fried with tofu,
    55–57
sole, fillets of, with zucchini and
    peppers, 64, 71–73
Sorosky, Marlene, 4
    menus of, 27–35
sorrel, 9
soufflé
    "old egg" with scallion and
        shrimp, 91, 98–100
    pumpkin, individual, 75, 80–81
soup
    California gazpacho, 82–85
    cream of lemon, 64, 71–73
    hearty vegetable chowder,
        75–77
    watercress, 47, 50–51
    wine "explosion" mushroom,
        with sweet peas, 91, 98–100
spaghetti squash
    with butter and Parmesan
        cheese, 35

with garden vegetable sauce,
    27, 33–35
    salad, 35
    with vegetables and diced
        chicken, 35
Spanish rice, 55, 58–60
spices, 14
    see also names of spices
spinach
    and mushrooms, braised, 64,
        69–70
    selection and storage of, 9
    stir-fried with glass noodles,
        91, 98–100
squash
    Louisiana-style mirlitons
        stuffed with ham and shrimp,
        36, 40–41
    pumpkin, see pumpkin
    selection and storage of, 10
    spaghetti squash
steamer, 12, 17 illus.
steaming, 11–12
stem vegetables
    selection and storage of, 9
    see also names of vegetables
stew, tofu, 91–93
stir-fried dishes
    curried pork with onions, 91,
        94–97
    rice with bell peppers and
        almonds, 91–93
    velvet spinach with glass
        noodles, 91, 98–100
stir-frying, 12–13
stock
    chicken, 13
    vegetable, 13
strawberries in liqueur with ice
    cream, 53
sugar, 15
summer squash, 10
sweet-and-sour sauce
    chicken breasts and vegetables
        with, 36, 42–45
    green beans with, 64–67
sweet potatoes, storage of, 9
Swiss chard, 9

Tamari, 56, 57
tart
    fruit, 32
    leek and mushroom, 75, 78–79
tofu, 15
    savory stew, 91–93
    stir-fried, with snow peas,
        55–57
tomatillos, 48, 49
tomatoes, 7, 15
    and cucumber with yogurt,
        22–23
    and mushrooms with chicken in
        parchment, 27–29
    and onion salad, 64–67
    with peas and beets, 25
    with peas and cumin seeds,
        24–25
    selection and storage of, 10
tomato paste, 15
tomato sauce

spicy, eggplant in, 18, 20–21
stuffed eggplant with, 82, 88–89
tossed green salad, 75–77
Tropp, Barbara, 5
menus of, 91–100
tuber vegetables
selection and storage of, 9
see also names of vegetables
turkey scallops with brown butter and caper sauce, 64–67
turmeric, 20

Vegetable oil, 14
vegetables
canned, 7, 9
with chicken breasts and sweet-and-sour sauce, 36, 42–45
classification of, 7, 9–10
cooking techniques, 11–13
cultivation, history of, 7
cutting techniques, 10–11
definition of, 7
frozen, 7–8, 9
health and, 8
selection of, 8–10
stock, 13
storage of, 9–10
wax coating on, 9
see also names of vegetables
vegetable steamer, 12, 17 illus.
vegetarian main dishes
artichoke frittata, 82–85
brown rice with mushrooms, 18, 24–25
chilies con queso (chilies with cheese fondue), 55, 58–60
deep-dish vegetable pot pies, 27, 30–32
eggplant pie, 36–39
hearty vegetable chowder, 75–77
leek and mushroom tart, 75, 78–79
pasta with mushroom sauce, 47, 52–53
Persian-style rice with lima beans and dill, 18, 22–23
puffed broccoli omelets, 55, 61–63
rice pilaf with black-eyed peas and green beans, 18–21
risotto with zucchini, 82, 86–87
saffron millet with stir-fried tofu and snow peas, 55–57
savory tofu stew, 91–93
spaghetti squash with garden vegetable sauce, 27, 33–35
stuffed eggplant with tomato sauce, 82, 88–89
velvet spinach with glass noodles, stir-fried, 91, 98–100
vinaigrette, herbed, green salad with, 36, 42–45
vinegars, 15

Watercress soup, 47, 50–51
wild rice with almonds, 55, 61–63
wine "explosion" mushroom soup with sweet peas, 91, 98–100

wines for flavoring, 15
winter squash, selection and storage of, 10

Yellow crookneck squash, 10
yellow onions, 9, 14
see also onions
yogurt
eggplant in, 18, 21
with mint, 18, 24–25
with tomato and cucumber, 18, 22–23

Zucchini
and peppers with fillets of sole, 64, 71–73
with risotto, 82, 86–87
selection and storage of, 10

Time-Life Books Inc. offers a wide range of fine recordings, including a Big Band series. For subscription information, call 1-800-621-7026, or write TIME-LIFE MUSIC, Time & Life Building, Chicago, Illinois 60611.